Palgrave Advances in Criminology and Criminal Justice in Asia

Series Editors
Bill Hebenton
Criminology & Criminal Justice
University of Manchester
Manchester, UK

Susyan Jou
School of Criminology
National Taipei University
Taipei, Taiwan

Lennon Y.C. Chang
School of Social Sciences
Monash University
Melbourne, Australia

This bold and innovative series provides a much needed intellectual space for global scholars to showcase criminological scholarship in and on Asia. Reflecting upon the broad variety of methodological traditions in Asia, the series aims to create a greater multi-directional, cross-national understanding between Eastern and Western scholars and enhance the field of comparative criminology. The series welcomes contributions across all aspects of criminology and criminal justice as well as interdisciplinary studies in sociology, law, crime science and psychology, which cover the wider Asia region including China, Hong Kong, India, Japan, Korea, Macao, Malaysia, Pakistan, Singapore, Taiwan, Thailand and Vietnam.

More information about this series at
http://www.palgrave.com/gp/series/14719

David T. Johnson

The Culture of Capital Punishment in Japan

David T. Johnson
University of Hawaii at Mānoa
Honolulu, HI, USA

Palgrave Advances in Criminology and Criminal Justice in Asia
ISBN 978-3-030-32085-0   ISBN 978-3-030-32086-7 (eBook)
https://doi.org/10.1007/978-3-030-32086-7

This title was first published in Japanese by Iwanami Shinsho, 2019 as "アメリカ人のみた日本
の死刑". [Amerikajin no Mita Nihon no Shikei]
© The Editor(s) (if applicable) and The Author(s) 2020. This book is an open access publication.
Open Access This book is licensed under the terms of the Creative Commons Attribution-NonCommercial-NoDerivatives 4.0 International License (http://creativecommons.org/licenses/by-nc-nd/4.0/), which permits any noncommercial use, sharing, distribution and reproduction in any medium or format, as long as you give appropriate credit to the original author(s) and the source, provide a link to the Creative Commons license and indicate if you modified the licensed material. You do not have permission under this license to share adapted material derived from this book or parts of it.
The images or other third party material in this book are included in the book's Creative Commons license, unless indicated otherwise in a credit line to the material. If material is not included in the book's Creative Commons license and your intended use is not permitted by statutory regulation or exceeds the permitted use, you will need to obtain permission directly from the copyright holder.
This work is subject to copyright. All commercial rights are reserved by the author(s), whether the whole or part of the material is concerned, specifically the rights of translation, reprinting, reuse of illustrations, recitation, broadcasting, reproduction on microfilms or in any other physical way, and transmission or information storage and retrieval, electronic adaptation, computer software, or by similar or dissimilar methodology now known or hereafter developed. Regarding these commercial rights a non-exclusive license has been granted to the publisher.
The use of general descriptive names, registered names, trademarks, service marks, etc. in this publication does not imply, even in the absence of a specific statement, that such names are exempt from the relevant protective laws and regulations and therefore free for general use.
The publisher, the authors and the editors are safe to assume that the advice and information in this book are believed to be true and accurate at the date of publication. Neither the publisher nor the authors or the editors give a warranty, expressed or implied, with respect to the material contained herein or for any errors or omissions that may have been made. The publisher remains neutral with regard to jurisdictional claims in published maps and institutional affiliations.

Cover credit: Alamy ACTG0F

This Palgrave Pivot imprint is published by the registered company Springer Nature Switzerland AG
The registered company address is: Gewerbestrasse 11, 6330 Cham, Switzerland

Preface

In July 2018, 13 former members of Aum Shinrikyo were executed in Japan, including Asahara Shoko, the guru of the new religion whose crimes killed at least 29 people and injured 6500 more. Aum's offenses were as heinous as any the country has seen. There was the premeditated slaughter of attorney Sakamoto Tsutsumi, his wife Satoko, and their infant son Tatsuhiko in Yokohama in 1989. There was the sarin gas attack in Matsumoto in 1994, which targeted judges overseeing a lawsuit involving Aum, and which killed eight people and injured more than 500. And there was Japan's crime of the century: a terrorist attack in which five coordinated releases of sarin gas in the Tokyo subway on March 20, 1995 killed 12 and injured more than 5500—and which (but for a bit of luck) could have killed many thousands.

No one was surprised when those Aum killers were condemned to death. In February 2004, I interviewed 30 of the people gathered on the sidewalks around the Tokyo District Court where Asahara was about to be sentenced to death. Everyone received the same question: "If Asahara is convicted, what sentence do you think is appropriate?" The ensuing conversations lasted six hours, with all but one respondent concluding that this serial killer deserved to die. The exception was an office lady who said she preferred a life sentence because "death would be too easy for him."

Fourteen years after Asahara was condemned to death, few Japanese objected when he and 12 of his henchman were hanged. Soon after those executions, Murakami Haruki (a well-known Japanese novelist) published an essay in a national newspaper which built on his moving accounts of the subway gas attacks that had been published two decades earlier.[1] In this essay, Murakami noted that "as a general argument, I adopt a stance of opposition toward the death penalty" but then said "I cannot publicly state, as far as this case is concerned, 'I am opposed to the death penalty'," because he had acquired "a painful awareness of the feelings of some bereaved families."[2]

By arguing that he opposes capital punishment *but not in this case*, Murakami is articulating a sensibility—the death penalty is "unavoidable" (*yamu o enai*)—that is ubiquitous in Japan's culture of capital punishment. Prosecutors use this expression to explain their charge decisions, to justify their demands for a death sentence, and to persuade Ministers of Justice to sign death warrants. Victims and survivors use it to lobby for the ultimate punishment. Reporters and editors use it to forecast capital outcomes and to interpret death sentences. Judges and lay judges use it—often—to explain and justify the death sentences they impose. And Japan's government uses it to ask citizens whether they support capital punishment (a typical survey question asks "Do you agree that the death penalty is unavoidable in some cases?"). The "unavoidable" expression simultaneously suggests that the death penalty "cannot be helped" and that the speaker is ambivalent about this purportedly "inescapable" outcome. The reservations wrapped in the expression suggest that Japanese capital punishment continues to operate because agents of the state (prosecutors, judges, politicians) and citizen-onlookers represent themselves, to themselves and others, as cogs in a machine over which they have little control.

Sociologically speaking, the view that capital punishment is "unavoidable" is a fiction—but it is a fiction that performs important functions. Claims that capital punishment "cannot be helped" provide comfort and deniability, both to those who participate in state killing, and to those who support and acquiesce to it. In this way, the linguistic formula reflects "bad faith" of the kind lamented by philosophers and

---

[1] Murakami's books *Andaguraundo* (Kodansha, 1997) and *Yakusoku Sareta Basho de* (Bungei Shunjusha, 1998) were published in English as *Underground: The Tokyo Gas Attack and the Japanese Psyche* (Vintage, 2000).

[2] Murakami Haruki, "AUM Shinrikyo Cases Still Not Closed", *The Mainichi*, July 29, 2018, at https://mainichi.jp/english/articles/20180729/p2a/00m/0na/004000c.

sociologists, for it "pretends something is necessary that in fact is voluntary."³ The frequent use of this fiction also illustrates how Japan's death penalty is kept "smothered under padded words," which modern societies frequently do in order to discourage debate about the subject.⁴

Systems of capital punishment ask normal people to perform extraordinary, prohibited acts—acts of bureaucratic, premeditated killing.⁵ To facilitate such acts, and to foster support for this form of state killing, Japan's culture of capital punishment provides a handy linguistic mechanism of moral disengagement. By framing capital punishment as "inevitable and unavoidable" (*yamu o enai*), this fiction disavows personal responsibility while lubricating the machinery of death and legitimating executions. In this era of abolition, when it has become increasingly difficult to defend capital punishment, these are noteworthy functions.

Many Japanese observers believe the Aum executions are exemplary, because the death penalty was "properly" imposed and "properly" carried out for murderous acts of breathtaking wickedness, and because the agony and anger of victims and survivors demanded that the ultimate penalty be paid. In these respects, the Aum executions give us a glimpse of the death penalty at its most legitimate. But on closer inspection, these executions—the best-case scenario for Japanese capital punishment—are deeply problematic. To wit:

- The Aum executions foreclosed many avenues for learning the truth about how promising young scientists became hardened killers.
- The executions leave lasting questions about why Hayashi Ikuo—the Aum executive who hoped to kill hundreds by releasing sarin gas on the Chiyoda subway line—escaped the ultimate punishment (he received a sentence of life imprisonment). Did his killings not qualify as the "worst of the worst"?
- The Aum executions failed to create "closure" for victims and survivors. For those whose bodies and souls have been brutalized,

---

³Peter L. Berger, *Invitation to Sociology: A Humanistic Perspective* (Anchor Books, 1963), p. 143.

⁴Albert Camus, "Reflections on the Guillotine", in *Resistance, Rebellion, and Death* (Vintage, 1960), p. 178.

⁵Craig Haney, *Death by Design: Capital Punishment as a Social Psychological System* (Oxford University Press, 2005), p. x.

a renewed sense of meaning and connection will only come (if it comes at all) from outside the law—from attachments with other people.
- The executions, which took place 23 years after the last Aum offenses, hardly send a credible message of deterrence to potential offenders who (research shows) are far more sensitive to the certainty and speed of punishment than to its severity.
- The executions leave lingering doubt about important legal issues, including the mental health of Asahara, who drooled and defecated on himself for years preceding his hanging, and whose appeal was never heard by Japan's Supreme Court.[6]
- The executions and the narrow focus on the individual responsibility of those who were hanged deflected attention from questions about the colossal failure of Japanese police to prevent the subway gas attack, despite an abundance of evidence that Aum was manufacturing sarin gas (among other weapons of mass destruction), and that Aum had used it some nine months before the attacks in Tokyo.
- And in a sharp and unexplained break from the customary practice of shrouding Japanese executions with secrecy and silence, the Aum executions were covered in real time by Japan's mass media, with reporters broadcasting from outside the gallows at the Tokyo Detention Center on the morning of July 6, and with television celebrities providing breathless hanging-by-hanging commentary for millions of viewers who tuned in on that day to sensationalistic stories about Japan's most notorious offenders *who-are-right-now-while-you-are-watching-finally-being-kicked-off-the-planet* ("and now a word from our sponsors"). That surreal media coverage maximized public enjoyment of death penalty discourse while minimizing public exposure to actual state killing, for no private citizens, no reporters, no victims, no survivors, and no family or friends of the condemned were allowed to attend any of the Aum executions.

---

[6]Japan has long been criticized for executing inmates with mental illness. See, for example, Amnesty International, "Hanging by a Thread: Mental Health and the Death Penalty in Japan", September 10, 2009, pp. 1–76; and *The Lancet*, "Execution of Prisoners with Mental Illnesses in Japan", Vol. 374, No. 9693 (September 12, 2009), p. 852.

In short, the seemingly exemplary execution of 13 Aum offenders in the summer of 2018 actually revealed much that is *wrong* with capital punishment in Japan.[7] It also raised a question that has long been ignored. The novelist Murakami wrote that he was willing to allow capital punishment for individuals who have committed heinous crimes, and many of his readers surely had a "me too" reaction. But acquiescence to the death penalty for a select few offenders seems myopic and naïve, for to employ the penalty of death at all is to presuppose the existence of a *system* of capital punishment that has far-reaching consequences. The pivotal question about capital punishment is not whether Aum offenders such as Asahara Shoko and Nakagawa Tomomasa deserve to die. The pivotal question is whether it is possible to construct a *system* of capital punishment that reaches *only* the rare right cases *without* also condemning the innocent or the undeserving.[8] This book argues that the answer is no.

Honolulu, USA   David T. Johnson

---

[7]On Aum's crimes and their criminal justice consequences, see Mori Tatsuya, *A3* (Shueisha Intanashunaru, 2010), and Nempo Shikei Haishi 2018, *Oumu Shikeishu kara Anata e* (Impakuto, 2018). And on the problems with seemingly "exemplary executions" in the United States, see David Garland, *Peculiar Institution: America's Death Penalty in an Age of Abolition* (The Belknap Press of Harvard University Press, 2010), pp. 1–8.

[8]Scott Turow, *Ultimate Punishment: A Lawyer's Reflections on Dealing with the Death Penalty* (Farrar, Straus and Giroux, 2003), p. 114.

Acknowledgements

I have been doing research about capital punishment in Japan for 15 years, and about criminal justice in Japan for 30. Thanks to all who have helped. You are a multitude. I have benefitted especially from the words and works of these scholars, journalists, attorneys, and friends: Adrienne Birch, Malcolm Feeley, Daniel H. Foote, Taku Fukada, Sayuri Furukawa, David Garland, Sadato Goto, Makoto Ibusuki, Naoko Iwakawa, Takeshi Kaneko, Koichi Kikuta, Setsuo Miyazawa, Kenji Nagata, Tomomasa Nakagawa, Kana Sasakura, Satoru Shinomiya, Maiko Tagusari, Akiko Takada, Takashi Takano, Masahiro Takeda, Scott Turow, Yoshihiro Yasuda, and Franklin E. Zimring. At Palgrave, I thank Josie Taylor and Liam Inscoe-Jones for their editorial support, and three anonymous reviewers who provided helpful comments. A Japanese version of this book was published by Iwanami Shinsho in May 2019, as *Amerikajin no Mita Nihon no Shikei* ["An American Perspective on Capital Punishment in Japan", translated by Kana Sasakura]. I would especially like to thank Professor Sasakura for her many valuable contributions, and Iwanami editors Noriyuki Shimamura and Yukiko Hori for their help during the years this project was in gestation.

PRAISE FOR *THE CULTURE OF CAPITAL PUNISHMENT IN JAPAN*

"This superb book, by an eminent scholar of criminal justice, provides many original insights about capital punishment in Japan. I welcome its publication, and I hope it moves Japan closer to abolition by informing readers in the rest of the world about the problems that afflict the death penalty in my country, and about the impossibility of administering capital punishment in a manner that is fair, just, and accurate."
—Koichi Kikuta, *Professor Emeritus, Meiji University*

"There is a saying in the board game of *Go* that 'on-lookers see more than players.' In this insightful book, David Johnson analyzes Japanese capital punishment from a variety of external perspectives. He also identifies obstacles to abolition, and he illuminates a path forward as well."
—Sadato Goto, *Attorney at Law, Osaka*

"David Johnson brings two rare capacities to this masterful essay—a deep and sympathetic knowledge of the law and culture of the Japanese criminal process, and an expert's understanding that civilizing state killing as a legal punishment is an impossibility in Japan or any other nation."
—Franklin E. Zimring, *Simon Professor of Law, University of California at Berkeley, USA*

"This brilliant book sheds light on many mysteries concerning Japan's machinery of death. It is the most interesting and provocative work on the subject. By combining empirical and sociological analysis, it shows how Japan's death penalty is peculiar in its own way, and it reveals troubling truths about Japanese criminal justice more generally."
—Kana Sasakura, *Professor of Law, Konan University*

"Japan's death penalty is shrouded in secrecy, because the Japanese government refuses to disclose many details about it. But this book lets the world know many disturbing realities. Its greatest achievement is that it reveals the reality of barbarous hangings in Japan—and of many other problems that plague Japanese capital punishment. Our NGO, 'Forum 90', recommends that this book be read widely in the United States and around the world. We have been calling for the abolition of Japanese capital punishment since 1990, and we request support from the rest of the world in pursuing this objective."
—Forum 90 for the ratification of the Second Optional Protocol to the International Covenant on Civil and Political Rights, aiming at the Abolition of the Death Penalty (http://forum90.net)

Contents

1 Why Does Japan Retain Capital Punishment?   1

2 Is Death Different? Two Ways Law Can Fail   19

3 When the State Kills in Secret   37

4 Wrongful Convictions and the Culture of Denial   61

5 Capital Punishment and Lay Participation   81

6 The Death Penalty and Democracy   101

Index   121

CHAPTER 1

Why Does Japan Retain Capital Punishment?

Abstract Japan retains the death penalty for three main reasons: because it missed a major opportunity for abolition in the postwar Occupation, because of the long hegemony of the (conservative) Liberal Democratic Party, and because (like the United States and China) it has sufficient size, economic influence, and political clout to enable it to defy human rights norms. Capital punishment also persists in Japan because it performs welcome functions for politicians, prosecutors, media, and the public. Despite widespread belief to the contrary, capital punishment in Japan does not deter homicide better than long terms of imprisonment do.

Keywords Karenina principle · Politics of retention · Abolition · Deterrence · *Via negativa* (negative path)

Leo Tolstoy's *Anna Karenina* (1878) begins by observing that "All happy families are alike, but each unhappy family is unhappy in its own way." On this view, for a marriage to be happy it must succeed in several ways, while failure in a single respect may mean a marriage is doomed. The "Karenina principle" has been applied in many fields, from business entrepreneurship and the domestication of animals to ecology and ethics. In some human activities, success requires avoiding many separate causes of failure.

There is a parallel with respect to capital punishment, for "abolitionist nations all seem alike, but every death penalty nation is retentionist in its own way."[1] On this version of the Karenina principle, abolition can fail for many reasons. Much has been written about why the United States retains capital punishment—and about why abolition has failed in this Western democracy when it has succeeded in every other one.[2] Some analysts emphasize the legacy of slavery and the role of "vigilante values," especially in the American south, where capital punishment is most commonly used.[3] Others stress the decentralized nature of American government, which makes it difficult to exercise national leadership on controversial questions of law and policy.[4] Still others argue that death penalty decisions by the U.S. Supreme Court diverted the country from the path of human rights that was followed by the developed democracies of Europe.[5] From this perspective, America would be abolitionist today if the Supreme Court had not declared in *Furman v. Georgia* in 1972 that capital punishment was unconstitutional because law failed to provide jurors with adequate guidance about how to exercise their sentencing discretion in life-or-death cases. The *Furman* decision also held that if states revised their laws to give jurors better guidance, the new capital punishment regimes could be constitutional. In this way, *Furman* triggered legal reforms and the resurgence of capital punishment in many American states. Conversely, if the U.S. Supreme Court had not intervened in this way, American capital punishment might have continued to wither away (there were no executions in the country from 1967 until *Furman* was reversed by the Supreme Court's *Gregg v. Georgia* decision

---

[1] David Garland, *Peculiar Institution: America's Death Penalty in an Age of Abolition* (The Belknap Press of Harvard University Press, 2010), p. 22.

[2] On explanations for America's death penalty exceptionalism, see Moshik Temkin, "The Great Divergence: The Death Penalty in the United States and the Failure of Abolition in Transatlantic Perspective", Harvard University Kennedy School of Government Faculty Research Working Paper Series, 2015, pp. 1–65, at https://www.hks.harvard.edu/publications/great-divergence-death-penalty-united-states-and-failure-abolition-transatlantic.

[3] Franklin E. Zimring, *The Contradictions of American Capital Punishment* (Oxford University Press, 2003).

[4] Andrew Hammel, *Ending the Death Penalty: The European Experience in Global Perspective* (Palgrave Macmillan, 2010).

[5] Carol S. Steiker and Jordan M. Steiker, *Courting Death: The Supreme Court and Capital Punishment* (The Belknap Press of Harvard University Press, 2016).

in 1976). On this view, there is nothing inevitable about America's continued commitment to capital punishment. Retention has been a contingent outcome, and history could have turned out differently.[6]

This book focuses on how Japan is "retentionist in its own way." It is based on my fieldwork in Japan over the past 30 years and on my reading of many works by journalists, legal professionals, and scholars about the death penalty in Japan and other countries.[7] My analysis of Japan's culture of capital punishment reveals that this developed democracy handles the gravest issue in criminal law in ways that are deeply problematic. The rest of this chapter explains why Japan retains capital punishment, and it debunks the belief that capital punishment in Japan deters homicide better than long terms of imprisonment do. Chapter 2 then shows

---

[6] Evan J. Mandery, *A Wild Justice: The Death and Resurrection of Capital Punishment in America* (W. W. Norton, 2013).

[7] There is a large literature on capital punishment in Japan in the Japanese language. Interested and able readers may find these works especially instructive: Kikuta Koichi, *Shikei: Sono Kyoko to Fujori* (Meiseki Shoten, 1999); Mori Tatsuya, *Shikei: Hito wa Hito o Koroseru. Demo Hito wa, Hito o Sukuitai tomo Omou* (Asahi Shimbunsha, 2008); Aoki Osamu, *Koshukei* (Kodansha, 2009); Horikawa Keiko, *Shikei no Kijun: "Nagayama Saiban" ga Nokoshita Mono* (Nihon Hyoronsha, 2009); Mori Honoo, *Naze Nihonjin wa Sekai no Naka de Shikei o Ze to Suru no ka: Kawariyuku Shikei Kijun to Kokumin Kanjo* (Gentosha, 2011); Yomiuri Shimbun Shakaibu, *Shikei: Kyukyoku no Batsu no Shinjitsu* (Chuo Koronshinsha, 2013); Sato Daisuke, *Shikei ni Chokumen Suru Hitotachi: Nikusei kara Mita Jittai* (Iwanami Shoten, 2016); and the *Nempo Shikei Haishi* ("Annual Report on the Abolition of Capital Punishment") series, which is published by Impakuto Press in Tokyo. Forum 90 (*Shikei Haishi Kokusai Joyaku no Hijun o Motomeru Forum 90*), Japan's largest abolitionist organization, publishes an informative newsletter ("Chikyu ga Kimeta Shikei Haishi") and webpage (http://forum90.net/). Forum 90's headquarters is in the Minato Godo Horitsu Jimusho law office of Yasuda Yoshihiro, in Tokyo. Yasuda, who worked as Asahara Shoko's lead defense lawyer and who has been one of Japan's abolitionist leaders since the 1980s, has written a fascinating memoir about his own death penalty work and activism: *Shikei Bengonin: "Ikiru" to Iu Kenri* (Kodansha, 2008). For representations of capital punishment in Japanese popular culture that explore various values and positions, see the *manga* series *Mori no Asagoe* (written by Gouda Mamora and published by Futabasha, 2005–2010), and the *manga*-based "Mori no Asagoe" television series that was originally broadcast on TV Tokyo and that is now available on DVD (Asmik Ace Entertainment, 2011). For a pro-death penalty book by a prison inmate who is serving a life sentence for murder, see Mitatsu Yamato, *Shikei Zettai Koteiron: Mukichoekishu no Shucho* (Shinchosha, 2010). And for works about death sentencing standards and execution methods by a scholar who supports capital punishment, see Kansai University Professor Nagata Kenji's website at https://penology.jimdo.com/.

that Japan's jurisprudence of capital punishment does not treat death as a "different" (*tokubetsu*) form of punishment requiring special procedures and protections for criminal defendants. Chapter 3 explains how and why the Japanese state kills in secret. Chapter 4 examines a culture of denial in Japanese criminal justice that produces wrongful convictions but makes their discovery difficult. Together, Chapters 2–4 help explain why there has been little reform in Japanese capital punishment over the past several decades.[8] When death is not deemed to be a different form of punishment, judges seldom find reason to worry about how the death penalty is administered, and legislators see little need to push for reform. When the state kills in secret, few people learn about the awful realities of execution, and fewer still perceive a need to change execution methods. And when the possibility of error in criminal justice decision-making is denied, complacency reigns supreme. After providing this account of stasis in Japanese capital punishment, Chapter 5 explores the prospects for change that could be stimulated by two new forms of citizen participation in the criminal process: the lay judge reform, and the victim participation system. Both of these reforms are less than a decade old, so it will take more time to discern their full effects, but so far the evidence suggests they may be doing more to entrench capital punishment than to dismantle or downsize it. Chapter 6 concludes by analyzing the loose links between public opinion and political leadership in Japanese capital punishment. It argues that a "democratic" approach to death penalty policymaking requires more than majority rule. Humans are not good at predicting the future (and experts are little better than amateurs),[9] but my own view is that in the long run there will be reforms which permanently deprive the Japanese state of the authority to kill its own citizens. If this happens, a variety of benefits will likely follow, as the concluding pages of this book suggest.

---

[8] David T. Johnson, "Retention and Reform in Japanese Capital Punishment", *University of Michigan Journal of Law Reform*, Vol. 49, No. 4 (Summer 2016), pp. 853–889; and David T. Johnson, *Koritsu Suru Nihon no Shikei* (Gendaijinbunsha, 2012, translated by Tagusari Maiko).

[9] Philip E. Tetlock, *Expert Political Judgment: How Good Is It? How Can We Know?* (Princeton University Press, 2005).

The Puzzle of Japanese Retention

In worldwide perspective, the most striking death penalty trend is decline.[10] As of 2019, more than two-thirds of the countries in the world have abolished the death penalty in law or practice, and the large majority of executions take place in only a handful of countries—China, North Korea, Iran, Iraq, and Saudi Arabia. A few countries have been carrying out executions more frequently in recent years (including Iran, Pakistan, and Vietnam), and a few others have been sentencing more people to death (Egypt and Nigeria), but the overall trend toward abolition is clear. In the United States as well, nine states have abolished capital punishment since 2007, and death sentences and executions have fallen to their lowest levels in a quarter-century.[11] In Texas, which has carried out more executions since 1976 than the next six most frequent executing states combined, executions have dropped dramatically, there have been fewer than 5 death sentences per year in recent years, and the size of the state's death row has declined by more than 40 percent since 1999. In 2017, just 3 counties out of more than 3000 in the nation accounted for more than 30 percent of America's 39 death sentences. In the same year, Harris County (Houston), Texas, which long was known as the "capital of capital punishment," imposed no death sentences and carried out no executions for the first time in 40 years.

In the context of all this death penalty decline, Japan's retention of capital punishment is puzzling in several respects. For starters, Japan is, with the United States, one of only a few developed democracies that retain capital punishment and continue to carry out executions on a regular basis. Most other rich and democratic countries have abolished the death penalty in law (Canada, Australia, New Zealand, and all the countries of Europe except the dictatorship of Belarus) or practice (South Korea last executed in 1997, and the last execution in Hong Kong occurred in 1966). But Japan does not have a decentralized democracy of the kind that has made abolition difficult in the United States,

---

[10] David T. Johnson, "A Factful Perspective on Capital Punishment", *Journal of Human Rights Practice* (2019, forthcoming).

[11] Death penalty developments in America and the world are summarized at https://deathpenaltyinfo.org/.

nor does it have a history of race relations like that which has shaped the death penalty in America. Conversely, Japan does have many of the structural characteristics that help explain the abolition of capital punishment in European countries such as Germany, France, and the United Kingdom, including a centralized state, a uniform penal code, a multi-party parliamentary system which helps insulate elected representatives from public opinion, and a civil law system with bureaucratic professionalization of the judiciary and the procuracy.[12] Despite these significant similarities, Japan has not converged toward abolitionist Europe in death penalty policy or practice.

The puzzle of Japanese retention deepens when one considers the two political circumstances that precipitated abolition in Western Europe after World War II, for those circumstances can also be found in recent Japanese history. In Germany, Italy, Portugal, and Spain, the fall of an authoritarian leader (Hitler, Mussolini, Salazar, and Franco) led to the abolition of the death penalty in 1944, 1949, 1976, and 1978, respectively. But after Japan's authoritarian political system collapsed in 1945, the death penalty did not disappear. Similarly, in Austria, Great Britain, and France, the election of a left-liberal government led to the abolition of capital punishment in 1950, 1965, and 1981, respectively.[13] But after the Democratic Party of Japan (DPJ) took control of Japan's central government in 2009, the death penalty was neither abolished nor significantly reformed.

Japanese retention also seems strange in light of two social facts connected to capital punishment in studies of the United States. First, Japan's homicide rate is about one-tenth the homicide rate for the United States and is lower than the homicide rates in all the abolitionist countries of Europe. In transatlantic comparisons, America's high murder rate is often invoked to explain why it retains capital punishment while European nations do not. On this explanation, the fear and outrage that murder inspires and that fuel public support for capital punishment are far more prevalent in the United States, where homicide is more

[12] Andrew Hammel, *Ending the Death Penalty: The European Experience in Global Perspective* (Palgrave Macmillan, 2010).
[13] Franklin E. Zimring, *The Contradictions of American Capital Punishment* (Oxford University Press, 2003).

common.[14] Yet this logic cannot explain retention in Japan, a country that has long had one of the lowest homicide rates in the world.[15]

The other social fact concerns inequality. In Japan, socioeconomic inequality grew after the economic bubble burst in 1990, but Japan remains more equal than America, where racial and social disparities help explain several death penalty facts, including the retention of the institution, the number of capital sentences and executions, and their geographical distribution.[16] Japan is like the United States and other death penalty nations in that the people most likely to be condemned to death and executed are poor and poorly connected, but inequality cannot explain the failure of abolition in this country.

THE POLITICS OF JAPANESE RETENTION

What, then, does explain the retention of capital punishment in Japan? The most persuasive explanations for the death penalty's trajectory focus on *state* institutions and the political and cultural processes that bear on *state* action.[17] The death penalty is always and everywhere an exercise of state power, and one must attend to the nature of the state and the contexts of state action in order to understand stability and change in any death penalty system. In the present case, a focus on the Japanese *state* produces three insights about the puzzle of retention in Japan.

First, Japan has the death penalty now partly because it missed a major opportunity for abolition in the postwar Occupation.[18] As described above, the death penalty was abolished in several nations of Europe shortly after authoritarian regimes fell. Similar abolitions have occurred in Asia too: in Cambodia after the fall of the Khmer Rouge (1989), in the Philippines after Marcos was overthrown (1987), and in East Timor

---

[14] Scott Turow, *Ultimate Punishment: A Lawyer's Reflections on Dealing with the Death Penalty* (Farrar, Straus and Giroux, 2003), p. 42.

[15] Dag Leonardsen, *Crime in Japan: Paradise Lost?* (Palgrave Macmillan, 2010).

[16] Charles J. Ogletree and Austin Sarat, editors, *From Lynch Mobs to the Killing State: Race and the Death Penalty in America* (New York University Press, 2006).

[17] David Garland, *Peculiar Institution: America's Death Penalty in an Age of Abolition* (The Belknap Press of Harvard University Press, 2010), p. 127.

[18] David T. Johnson, "Why Does Japan Retain the Death Penalty? Nine Hypotheses", in Lill Scherdin, editor, *Capital Punishment: A Hazard to a Sustainable Criminal Justice System?* (Ashgate, 2014), p. 141.

after it gained independence from Indonesia (1999). In these countries, abolition was a way of symbolically distancing new governments from the state killing performed by their predecessors. Japan experienced regime change following its surrender in 1945, but the death penalty endured throughout the subsequent process of state transformation even though the reform agenda in the America-led occupation was highly ambitious. That agenda included land reform, gender equality, new rights for criminal suspects and defendants, and the downsizing of the emperor from god to a mere mortal. But capital punishment was not a reform priority. This distinguishes the occupation of Japan from the parallel occupation of Germany (which abolished the death penalty in 1949), and it also helps explain why Japan remains retentionist today. One key part of this retentionist story is the desire of American officials to condemn Japanese "war criminals" to death in the Tokyo War Crimes Trial (seven persons were executed in 1948). When a country is defeated in war, the desire to exact revenge against leaders of the losing regime can cause capital punishment to become more durable than it otherwise would be. The hanging of Saddam Hussein in 2006 and the subsequent resurgence of executions in Iraq illustrates the continued relevance of this possibility.

Second, the persistence of capital punishment in Japan after the occupation ended can be explained by the long and conservative hegemony of the Liberal Democratic Party and by the inability of other political parties to change death penalty policy and practice when they briefly controlled government.[19] The LDP gained control of Japan's central government in 1955, three years after the Occupation ended. Over the following 60 years it maintained control for all but 50 months. The first interregnum lasted only 8 months (in 1993–1994), and the coalition government of seven parties was too brief and fractious to enable reform of capital punishment. The second interruption of LDP rule started in August 2009, when the Democratic Party of Japan gained control of central government and kept it until it lost power in the landslide election of December 2012. In this period, too, there was no move toward abolition or a moratorium on executions despite DPJ promises to proceed more cautiously with capital punishment than the LDP had done. In 2010, after signing two execution

---

[19] David T. Johnson, "Why Does Japan Retain the Death Penalty? Nine Hypotheses", in Lill Scherdin, editor, *Capital Punishment: A Hazard to a Sustainable Criminal Justice System?* (Ashgate, 2014), p. 142.

warrants and attending those executions, DPJ Minister of Justice Chiba Keiko opened the gallows in Tokyo to select members of the media and formed a death penalty study team in her Ministry, but the gallows were not in use when reporters visited, the research team produced no concrete proposals for action on capital punishment, and Chiba provided no clear explanation for her decision to order executions after having publically opposed capital punishment during the quarter-century or so that she served in the Diet before becoming Minister. I will return to this episode in Chapter 6, where I discuss the relationship between public opinion and political leadership in death penalty policymaking. Two of Chiba's seven successors as Minister of Justice under the DPJ (Ogawa Toshio and Taki Makoto) also authorized executions. In total, these three Ministers ordered 16 executions during the 40 months of DPJ rule. European experience suggests that abolition is more likely to occur under the leadership of a liberal party than a conservative one (see Austria, Great Britain, and France), and something similar can be said of the recent moratoria on executions in South Korea and Taiwan.[20] In the United States as well, abolition has seldom occurred in conservative states, though in 2015 Nebraska did become the first predominantly Republican state to abolish the death penalty in 40 years. In comparative perspective, the durability of Japan's death penalty reflects not only the long-term hegemony of its ruling party but also the fact that the other parties that have held power were almost indistinguishable from the conservative LDP in their policy preferences and commitments. In short, conservative politics has contributed to the conservation of capital punishment in Japan.

The third aspect of my explanation of Japanese retention stresses the state's geopolitical position, especially in the years after 1980, when Japan emerged as an economic power. Like the United States, China, and India, Japan has sufficient size, economic influence, and political clout to make it difficult for external forces such as international law, human rights norms, and United Nations resolutions to impose meaningful sanctions for noncompliance.[21] Powerful states seldom cede to supranational entities; they tend to endorse international norms that

---

[20] David T. Johnson and Franklin E. Zimring, *The Next Frontier: National Development, Political Change, and the Death Penalty in Asia* (Oxford University Press, 2009), see especially Chapter 5 (on South Korea) and Chapter 6 (on Taiwan).

[21] Sangmin Bae, *When the State No Longer Kills: International Human Rights Norms and Abolition of Capital Punishment* (State University of New York Press, 2007).

serve their own purposes and reject those that do not. There are many examples of this selectivity: the United States' use of torture in the "war on terror," China's limits on freedom of expression, Japanese whaling, caste-based discrimination in India, and the retention of capital punishment in all of these countries. In these large nations, it is more difficult for the "human rights dynamic"[22] that has been driving abolition in many parts of the world to influence death penalty policy and practice than it is for the same dynamic to have an effect in Gabon, Latvia, Bolivia, Congo, Fiji, Madagascar, Suriname, Benin, Nauru, and Guinea, ten countries that have abolished capital punishment since 2010.

In many respects, Japan remains committed to a model of law and government that considers "self-sufficiency" a virtue and that resists and resents attempts at outside influence. Japan is also ruled (once again) by a Liberal Democratic Party, some of whose members believe that human rights are not universal. Of course, Japan does follow America's lead in some matters of foreign policy. Indeed, Japan's subordination in this sphere is sometimes so extreme that it has been called a "puppet state." In this sense, Japan's retention of capital punishment may depend on American retention, for when a superpower that sees itself as the archetypal liberal democracy continues to kill its own citizens, it provides cover and legitimacy for other nations that want to do the same. If the United States abolishes capital punishment, as some analysts predict,[23] Japan could continue to resist pressure to conform to the emerging norm of abolition, as it has done with respect to whaling ever since the International Whaling Commission's moratorium on commercial whaling went into effect in 1986. But in my view, a more likely response to American abolition would be for Japan to do what it has often done in its modern history: adapt to the changing circumstances of its external environment[24]—and abolish capital punishment. But of course, this possibility is premised on the big "if" of American abolition. As of 2019, that has not happened, and Japanese leaders perceive little pressure to abolish, either from foreign actors and abolitionists or from their own domestic

[22] Roger Hood and Carolyn Hoyle, "Abolishing the Death Penalty Worldwide: The Impact of a 'New Dynamic'", *Crime and Justice*, Vol. 38, No. 1 (2009), pp. 1–63.

[23] Charles J. Ogletree and Austin Sarat, editors, *The Road to Abolition? The Future of Capital Punishment in the United States* (New York University Press, 2009).

[24] Kenneth B. Pyle, *Japan Rising: The Resurgence of Japanese Power and Purpose* (Public Affairs, 2007).

constituencies. Unlike Europe, Asia has no regional organizations to nudge Japan toward abolition, as the European Union and the Council of Europe did to countries in Central and Eastern Europe after the Cold War ended. In the geopolitics of capital punishment, Asia is not Europe, and Japan is not Latvia or Lithuania.

Does the Death Penalty Deter Homicide in Japan?

Prosecutors, politicians, and the public frequently claim that the death penalty must be retained in Japan because it deters homicide.[25] But does it really perform this function?

In the United States, a blue-ribbon panel of scholars reviewed dozens of peer-reviewed studies on this subject, and they concluded that there is no good evidence that the death penalty deters homicide.[26] In Japan, a recent study focused on the period 1990–2010.[27] The study has two main strengths. First, it employs *monthly* homicide statistics instead of annual figures, which enables us to discern the consequences of death sentences and executions over time. Without monthly homicide data (which Japan's National Police Agency seldom releases), associations between fluctuations in homicide and capital punishment cannot be reliably discerned. Without monthly homicide figures, the annual homicide total (one number per year) provides too few data points to satisfy the assumptions of statistical models. And without monthly homicide data, statistical models of the death penalty and deterrence can only generate crude annual estimates.

The second strength of the Japan study is that it employs separate statistics for *homicide* and *robbery-homicide*, two kinds of killing that differ in crucial respects. In Japan, robbery-homicide is about 15 times less common than homicide. In Japan, robbery-homicide offenders are about 7 times less likely to know their victims. In Japan, robbery-homicide offenders are about 15 times more likely to be

---

[25] Petra Schmidt, *Capital Punishment in Japan* (Brill, 2002), pp. 102–113.

[26] National Research Council Committee on Deterrence and the Death Penalty, Daniel S. Nagin and John V. Pepper, editors, *Deterrence and the Death Penalty* (National Academies Press, 2012).

[27] Kanji Muramatsu, David T. Johnson, and Koiti Yano, "The Death Penalty and Homicide Deterrence in Japan", *Punishment & Society*, Vol. 20, No. 4 (October 2018), pp. 432–457.

motivated by greed. And in Japan, persons convicted of robbery-homicide are about 15 times more likely to be sentenced to death than persons convicted of homicide. These differences in frequency, motivation, context, and the severity of punishment make robbery-homicide the best possible crime candidate for finding a deterrent effect from the death penalty. Yet even for this thin slice of heinous murder, there was no discernible deterrent effect from death sentences or executions—nor was there a deterrent effect on homicide more generally.

In short, the best available evidence suggests that death sentences and executions do not deter homicide or robbery-homicide in Japan. This double-negative is striking because Japanese criminal justice punishes robbery-homicide harshly, and because robbery-homicide is a crime of calculation. This finding is also consistent with findings about the death penalty and deterrence in other countries—including Singapore, which long was the world's most aggressive executing state[28]—and with crime and capital punishment patterns in postwar Japan.[29] Japan's homicide rate has declined by more than 80 percent since the 1950s.[30] Over the same period, Japan's annual execution average dropped from 25 hangings per year in the decade of the 1950s to less than 5 per year in the 2000s—a decline of more than 80 percent during a period in which the country's population grew more than 50 percent. Killers have been vanishing in Japan, especially young male killers, who currently commit (per capita) approximately one-tenth as many homicides as their youthful counterparts did in the 1950s.[31] In fact, at present Japan's homicide rate is higher among men in their 50s than among men in their 20s—an age-crime distribution seldom seen in other societies. It may be possible to construct an explanation for Japan's vanishing young killer that posits capital punishment as a signal to which young males are especially

---

[28] Franklin E. Zimring, Jeffrey Fagan, and David T. Johnson, "Executions, Deterrence, and Homicide: A Tale of Two Cities", *Journal of Empirical Legal Studies*, Vol. 7, No. 1 (March 2010), pp. 1–29.

[29] See David T. Johnson and Franklin E. Zimring, *The Next Frontier: National Development, Political Change, and the Death Penalty in Asia* (Oxford University Press, 2009), especially Chapter 3 (on Japan).

[30] David T. Johnson, "Comparative Reflections on American Crime Declines", *Berkeley Journal of Criminal Law*, No. 23-3 (Fall 2018), pp. 25–45.

[31] David T. Johnson, "The Homicide Drop in Postwar Japan", *Homicide Studies*, Vol. 12, No. 1 (February 2008), pp. 146–160.

sensitive, but such an explanation would seem to contradict the general criminological truth that criminal risk-taking tends to decline with age.

There are two more points to emphasize about the death penalty and deterrence. First, after publication of the article cited in footnote 27, Japanese officials cannot credibly claim there is empirical evidence to support the view that the death penalty deters homicide—though they might continue to contend that "common sense" leads to their preferred conclusion. Once upon a time, "common sense" also held that the earth is flat. Second, in abolitionist countries, evidence about deterrence has been largely irrelevant to the ultimate decision about whether to retire the executioner. Decisions to abolish are determined mainly by political developments and moral sentiments, not by utilitarian considerations. Japan does not *need* the death penalty in order to prevent homicide. The question its leaders and citizens need to confront is why they *want* a sanction that is unnecessary for public protection. Is it to reflect public opinion, which is ill-informed by the policies of secrecy and silence that surround capital punishment? Is it to serve victims, which makes application of the ultimate penalty depend on the intensity of survivors' anger? Or does Japan retain the death penalty mainly to achieve retribution, which is often a form of vengeance-in-disguise? Calls for revenge form one of the least discussed but most powerful forces in Japan's continued use of capital punishment. Should its political leaders indulge demands for vengeance, as they have increasingly done in recent years, or should they try to tame such impulses because they are dangerous and undemocratic? I will return to these questions in the final two chapters of this book.

Conclusion

There is a triumphalist tone in much writing about capital punishment. Some of it is in response to the truly remarkable progress toward abolition that has occurred in the world, and some of it is in anticipation of a future that is believed to hold the certainty of abolition everywhere. According to some prominent analysts, "great progress" has been made toward worldwide abolition of capital punishment,[32] and "it seems

---

[32] Roger Hood and Carolyn Hoyle, "Progress Made for Worldwide Abolishment of Death Penalty", *International Affairs Forum: Capital Punishment Around the World*, Vol. 6, No. 1 (Summer 2015), p. 8.

nothing can stop continued progress towards universal abolition."[33] I would like to see abolition spread further, and I favor reforms that would restrict the scope and scale of capital punishment in Japan. I also believe that, eventually, Japan will abolish. But in death penalty scholarship there have been few serious studies of *failures of abolition*.[34] This chapter has explained the failure of abolition in Japan, one of three major democracies in the world that retain capital punishment (along with the United States and India). I have stressed the importance of *state* institutions and the political and cultural processes that bear on *state* action. I do not claim that Japan retains capital punishment because Japanese people support it, for as explained in Chapter 6, the experience of other countries shows that public opposition to capital punishment is not a necessary condition for abolition. When the leaders of a country decide to abolish the death penalty, they do so despite majority public support for the institution—and they do so to get on "the right side of history."[35]

The case of Japan suggests that abolition might not be near in some societies. This insight is instructive in two ways. For one thing, there are contingencies and complexities in the future trajectory of capital punishment. For the foreseeable future, all roads do not necessarily lead to abolition. For another, a focus on Japan's failure of abolition may help death penalty opponents discern how to move toward reforms they favor by identifying obstacles to change. One challenge for Japanese abolitionists is how to make the language of "human rights" more relevant in a society where this framework is not as salient as in nations that have already abolished (as in Germany and South Africa) or moved toward abolition (as in South Korea and Taiwan). A second challenge is how to overcome the presumption among Japanese politicians that the public would not tolerate abolition. Research suggests that the

---

[33] William A. Schabas, "Universal Abolition of Capital Punishment Is Drawing Nearer", *International Affairs Forum: Capital Punishment Around the World*, Vol. 6, No. 1 (Summer 2015), p. 13.

[34] For an exception, see Moshik Temkin, "The Great Divergence: The Death Penalty in the United States and the Failure of Abolition in Transatlantic Perspective", Harvard University Kennedy School of Government Faculty Research Working Paper Series, 2015, pp. 1–65, at https://www.hks.harvard.edu/publications/great-divergence-death-penalty-united-states-and-failure-abolition-transatlantic.

[35] Kevin M. Barry, "The Law of Abolition", *Journal of Criminal Law & Criminology* (Fall 2017), p. 556.

Japanese public would accept abolition, and with little or no damage to legal legitimacy or political authority.³⁶ The third challenge for Japan's abolitionists is how to persuade politicians—especially those who are conservative—that Japan does not need the death penalty, for one lesson from developed democracies that have abolished the death penalty is that shifts in elite opinion are key. Public opinion on capital punishment is largely resistant to abolitionists' attempts to change it, and the straightest road to abolition may involve "bypassing public opinion entirely."³⁷

Focusing on how Japan "is retentionist in its own way" should also create curiosity about the positive effects of capital punishment, which many abolitionists ignore. The notion that capital punishment "represents the pointless and needless extinction of life with only marginal contributions to any discernible social or public purposes"³⁸ may be inspiring rhetoric to opponents of the death penalty, but it is bad sociology. So is the sweeping claim that "even when its aims are modest, capital punishment fails to achieve them."³⁹ As New York University Professor David Garland demonstrates in his masterful account of American capital punishment:

> If we insist...on a positive account of capital punishment's uses and utilities, even those that at first seem marginal or unimportant, then a picture emerges that turns the [abolitionists'] conventional wisdom upside down. What becomes apparent is that the state's power to kill is actually productive, performative, and generative – that it *makes things happen* – even if much of what happens is in the cultural realm of death penalty discourse rather than in the biological realm of life and death (emphasis in original).⁴⁰

In Japan, too, capital punishment persists partly because it performs positive functions. For prosecutors, it is a practical instrument that

---

³⁶ Mai Sato, *The Death Penalty in Japan: Will the Public Tolerate Abolition?* (Springer VS, 2014).

³⁷ Andrew Hammel, *Ending the Death Penalty: The European Experience in Global Perspective* (Palgrave Macmillan, 2010), p. 193.

³⁸ Justice John Paul Stevens in *Baze v Rees*, 553 U.S. 35, 85 (2008).

³⁹ Mario Marazziti, *13 Ways of Looking at the Death Penalty* (Seven Stories Press, 2015), p. 201.

⁴⁰ David Garland, *Peculiar Institution: America's Death Penalty in an Age of Abolition* (The Belknap Press of Harvard University Press, 2010), pp. 285–286.

enables them to harness the power of death in the pursuit of criminal convictions, harsh punishments, and public support. For politicians, it is a way to gain votes, stay in office, and receive publicity—that is, it is a tool to be used in electoral games that are played before viewing and voting audiences. For the media, it is a prurient entertainment and a morality play that pits good against evil. For the public, it is an opportunity to express emotions (such as anger, hatred, and vengeance) that normally are prohibited. And for victims and survivors of crime, capital punishment is believed to be a mechanism for achieving retribution, atonement, and deterrence. Although these beliefs are founded as much in faith as in fact, they are sociologically and practically significant because they are subjectively meaningful to the believers.[41]

In short, the retention of capital punishment in Japan stems partly from the positive functions it performs for various actors and audiences. Opponents of capital punishment would be wise to recognize this reality. At the same time, Japanese retention reflects what is *not* found in and around the institution of capital punishment. As I will show in the rest of this book, Japan has *not* operationalized the principle that death is a different kind of criminal punishment requiring special procedures and protections (Chapter 2). A lay judge panel can convict and condemn a defendant to death by a vote of 5 to 4. Does this reflect the "caution" about capital punishment that Ministers of Justice routinely emphasize in their post-execution pronouncements? Similarly, the Japanese state is *not* open about how it kills (Chapter 3). In fact, the main purpose of the secrecy surrounding Japanese executions is the protection of capital punishment from protest and criticism that would occur if executions were announced in advance. Is this transparent and democratic? And Japan has *not* discovered many wrongful convictions (Chapter 4). Is this because Japanese criminal justice produces few of them, or because the system is ill-equipped to find them? In all of these respects, what Japan does *not* do can be contrasted with the United

---

[41] The analysis in this paragraph echoes David Garland's analysis about the positive functions of American capital punishment in Chapter 11 ("Death and Its Uses") of his *Peculiar Institution* (2010). For an essay about Garland's magnificent book, see David T. Johnson, "American Capital Punishment in Comparative Perspective", *Law & Social Inquiry*, Vol. 36, No. 4 (Fall 2011), pp. 1033–1061.

States, where markedly more death penalty reform has occurred as the result of concerns about due process violations, botched executions, and the revelation of wrongful convictions.

Although Japan is retentionist "in its own way," there are some ways in which other retentionist countries resemble it. In Singapore, which long has employed one of the most aggressive death penalty systems in the world and which is far from a model of due process, an article in the country's leading law journal claims that "no sweeping reforms are necessary" to reduce the risk of wrongful conviction.[42] That claim is claptrap. In Taiwan, where the number of executions dropped dramatically as the country democratized but where executions have rebounded in recent years, death is not different as a matter of law or practice, and major mistakes have been made in the administration of capital punishment—including the wrongful execution of an innocent man (Chiang Kuo-ching), which Taiwan's government acknowledged in 2011.[43] And in the People's Republic of China, the world's biggest user of capital punishment, debate about the death penalty has deepened in recent years, yet its death penalty system remains shrouded in secrecy, including a prohibition on disclosing how many executions are performed each year.[44]

The Karenina principle suggests that success at abolishing capital punishment requires avoiding many separate causes of failure. It also implies that the road to abolition is not merely a positive path embracing the "human rights dynamic" and "leadership from the front" in the face of public support for capital punishment, though these have been important causes of change in many death penalty nations. The road to abolition is also a "negative path"—what the ancient Greeks called *via negativa*—leading away from doctrines and practices that present obstacles to ending the death penalty.[45]

---

[42] Chen Siyuan and Eunice Chua, "Wrongful Convictions in Singapore: A General Survey of Risk Factors", *Singapore Law Review*, Vol. 28 (2010), pp. 98–123.

[43] Cindy Sui, "Executed Taiwan Airman Chiang Kuo-ching Innocent", BBC News, September 13, 2011.

[44] David T. Johnson and Michelle Miao, "Chinese Capital Punishment in Comparative Perspective", in Bin Liang and Hong Lu, editors, *The Death Penalty in China: Policy, Practice, and Reform* (Columbia University Press, 2015), pp. 300–326.

[45] Rolf Dobelli, *The Art of Thinking Clearly* (Harper, 2013), p. 299.

As in the pursuit of happiness and professional success, so too, perhaps, in the pursuit of a world free from state killing: negative knowledge (what not to do) can be as potent as positive knowledge (what to do). In the end, thinking about what makes Japan "retentionist in its own way" might have the welcome effect of improving our understanding of why the death penalty endures in one of the world's most developed countries.

Open Access This chapter is licensed under the terms of the Creative Commons Attribution-NonCommercial-NoDerivatives 4.0 International License (http://creativecommons.org/licenses/by-nc-nd/4.0/), which permits any noncommercial use, sharing, distribution and reproduction in any medium or format, as long as you give appropriate credit to the original author(s) and the source, provide a link to the Creative Commons license and indicate if you modified the licensed material. You do not have permission under this license to share adapted material derived from this chapter or parts of it.

The images or other third party material in this chapter are included in the chapter's Creative Commons license, unless indicated otherwise in a credit line to the material. If material is not included in the chapter's Creative Commons license and your intended use is not permitted by statutory regulation or exceeds the permitted use, you will need to obtain permission directly from the copyright holder.

CHAPTER 2

Is Death Different? Two Ways Law Can Fail

Abstract This chapter describes how capital cases are handled in Japan and the United States—the two largest developed democracies that retain capital punishment and continue to carry out executions on a regular basis. The comparison shows that death penalty law can fail in two ways. In the United States, where the Supreme Court has ruled that "death is different," law fails by not fulfilling many of its promises to provide special procedures and protections for capital defendants. In Japan, by contrast, law fails by not making many promises at all.

Keywords Capital jurisprudence · Death is different · Super due process · Factual accuracy · Moral accuracy · Legal failure

Despite frequent claims by Japanese officials to the contrary, Japan is not "careful" about how it administers capital punishment. In Japan, potentially capital cases are treated much the same as less serious cases. Yet if "a single life weighs more than the entire earth," as Japan's Supreme Court asserted in a 1948 decision upholding the constitutionality of capital punishment, then why doesn't Japanese criminal procedure reflect this reality?

This chapter describes how death penalty cases are treated in Japan and the United States, the two most prominent developed democracies that retain capital punishment and continue to use it on a regular basis.

© The Author(s) 2020
D. T. Johnson, *The Culture of Capital Punishment in Japan*,
Palgrave Advances in Criminology and Criminal Justice in Asia,
https://doi.org/10.1007/978-3-030-32086-7_2

The comparison shows that the law can fail in two ways. In the United States, law fails by not fulfilling many of its promises to provide special procedures and protections for defendants in capital cases. In Japan, law fails by not making any promises at all.

Is Japan Careful About Capital Punishment?

In the murder trial of Tateyama Tatsumi that took place in Chiba District Court in 2011, defense lawyers made two extraordinary appeals to the three professional judges and six lay judges who decided whether Tateyama should be condemned to death for the offenses—including one murder—that he committed during a two-month rampage which started two weeks after he was released from Tsukigata prison in Hokkaido, where he had served a seven-year sentence for robbery. On the first day of this trial, defense lawyer Urazaki Hiroyasu began his opening argument by telling the court that this would probably be a capital trial and that the people sitting in judgment should therefore pay careful attention to the proceedings which would follow. "The death penalty is an extremely severe punishment," Urazaki observed. "It ought to be used carefully, and it should only be imposed if it cannot possibly be avoided."

Two weeks later, on the last day of Tateyama's trial and a few minutes after prosecutors had stated for the first time that they wanted Tateyama sentenced to death, defense lawyer Murai Hiroaki asked the court to impose a capital sentence if and only if everyone on the panel agreed that death was the appropriate penalty. Under Japan's lay judge law, five votes are enough to convict a defendant and sentence him or her to death, a decision rule that Tateyama's defense team believed was insufficiently cautious. "The death penalty must be administered very carefully," Murai implored the court. "If you cannot reach a consensus, then please do not impose the ultimate penalty."

Urazaki's prediction proved prescient, and Murai's request was ignored. During the press conference following the trial session where Tateyama was sentenced to death, one lay judge wondered: "Is this really the right thing to do? I still have doubts" (*honto ni kore de yokatta no ka? mada gimon o motte iru*). But before he could describe the nature of his misgivings, this lay judge was stopped by a clerk of the court who had been assigned the role of enforcing the confidentiality clause of the Lay Judge Law, which allows dissent only if it remains secret. A similar but unwritten rule discourages dissent on Japan's Supreme Court when it finalizes a sentence of death.[1] The net effect of these policies of secrecy and silence is to dissuade public discussion about the gravest decision a government can make.

The arguments by Tateyama's defense lawyers were meant to encourage the Chiba court to be careful about employing death as a punishment. In the United States their requests would have been unnecessary because American prosecutors are required to tell defense lawyers and the court—long before a trial starts—whether they intend to seek a sentence of death, and because the decision rule in American capital trials is consensus: if even 1 juror out of 12 considers a capital sentence inappropriate, the defendant cannot be condemned to death.

In Japan, everyone associated with capital punishment—prosecutors, judges, lay judges, defense lawyers, Ministers of Justice, the media, politicians, and victims and survivors—acknowledges that life-and-death decisions should be made as "carefully" as possible (*shincho ni*), but the institutional and procedural reality is that capital cases are treated much the same as other criminal cases. In reality, death is not different in Japan.

"Death Is Different" in the United States

Since the 1970s, the U.S. Supreme Court has held that "death is different" from other criminal punishments in two respects. First, death is different in its severity and enormity, for as "the ultimate punishment" it denies the offender's humanity and the possibility of his or her reform. In addition, death is different because the finality of execution makes the consequences of error irreversible. The recognition that death is different in these ways has generated an array of special procedural protections for capital defendants. Most fundamentally, ordinary due process is not enough; there must be "super due process" (and international human rights law proceeds from a similar premise).

Super due process has five implications in American criminal procedure.[2] First, capital trials must be carried out in separate stages: first determining the guilt of a defendant, and then (if the defendant has

---

[1] Yamaguchi Susumu and Miyaji Yu, *Saikosai no Anto: Shosuiken ga Jidai o Kirihiraku* (Asahi, 2011), p. 51.

[2] Robert M. Bohm, *Ultimate Sanction: Understanding the Death Penalty Through Its Many Voices and Many Sides* (Kaplan Publishing, 2010), pp. vi–ix.

been convicted) deciding the sentence. Second, capital juries must be given direction in the form of "aggravating and mitigating factors" to help guide their discretion at the sentencing stage. Third, after a death sentence has been imposed it receives an automatic appellate review, regardless of the defendant's wishes. In some American jurisdictions, defendants who have been sentenced to death cannot waive their right to appeal, as approximately one-third of death-sentenced defendants in Japan do. Fourth, American appellate courts engage in proportionality review in order to identify inappropriate disparities in sentencing practice. The principle underlying this practice is that like cases should be treated alike, and different cases differently. Finally, in order to impose a capital sentence, all 12 jurors must agree that death is the appropriate sanction. For the defense this means that a sentence of death can be prevented by convincing just one juror to oppose it. Clarence Darrow, one of the most highly esteemed defense lawyers in American history, defended more than 100 persons in capital trials, and not a single one was sentenced to death.[3] But if Darrow had faced a majority rule like the one that prevails in Japan, he probably would have had a different record.

Although American law promises super due process, it often fails to deliver.[4] A classic study of error rates in American capital cases found that serious error—error substantially undermining the reliability of capital verdicts—had reached "epidemic proportions" in America's death penalty system. In this analysis, the "overall error rate" was defined as the proportion of fully reviewed capital judgments that were overturned on appeal due to serious error between 1973 and 1995. By this definition, the overall error rate was 68 percent, which means that approximately two out of every three capital sentences reviewed by appellate courts were reversed because they were found to be seriously flawed.[5] As of 2017, only 15 percent of all death

---

[3] John A. Farrell, *Clarence Darrow: Attorney for the Damned* (Vintage Books, 2011).

[4] Carol S. Steiker and Jordan M. Steiker, *Courting Death: The Supreme Court and Capital Punishment* (The Belknap Press of Harvard University Press, 2016), especially Chapter 5 ("The Failures of Regulation").

[5] James S. Liebman, Jeffrey Fagan, and Valerie West, "A Broken System: Error Rates in Capital Cases, 1973–1995", https://papers.ssrn.com/sol3/papers.cfm?abstract_id=232712.

sentences imposed by American trial courts since 1977 had resulted in execution. By state, the range runs from less than 1 percent in Pennsylvania to more than 70 percent in Virginia. The most common errors in American death penalty trials include police and prosecutors who suppressed exculpatory evidence or committed other professional misconduct, incompetent defense lawyers, jurors who were misinformed about the law, and biased judges and jurors. When America's appellate courts find serious error, more than 8 out of every 10 cases sent back for retrial end in a sentence less than death—and 9 percent end in acquittal. The fundamental cause of all of this error is overuse. "The more often officials use the death penalty," a subsequent study concluded, "the greater the risk that capital convictions and sentences will be seriously flawed."[6]

It is widely believed that Japan uses capital punishment less frequently than the United States, but this view is mistaken. In per capita terms (executions per million population), Japan's execution rate has long been lower than that for the United States, and it has been much lower than the rates in high-rate American states such as Texas and Virginia. But the per capita rate of execution is a poor measure of frequency of use because (Stalinist nightmares aside) persons are not selected randomly for death; they are condemned and executed from a larger pool of potentially capital cases. In the United States and Japan, this pool consists entirely of homicide crimes. Hence, to assess the scale of capital punishment in a country, one must consider the size of the relevant capital-crime pool. In the United States, about 2 percent of all known murder offenders are sentenced to death, though this figure varies by state, from around 0.4 percent in Colorado to 6 percent or so in Nevada. The probability of a known murderer being sentenced to death in Japan is not much different than in many American jurisdictions. From 1994 through 2003, the chance of a Japanese murderer being sentenced to death was 1.3 percent—about the same rate as in the American states of California and Virginia. And in 2007, when Japan had 14 death sentences in courts of

---

[6] James S. Liebman, Jeffrey Fagan, Andrew Gelman, Valerie West, Garth Davies, and Alexander Kiss, "A Broken System, Part II: Why There Is So Much Error in Capital Cases, and What Can Be Done About It", http://www2.law.columbia.edu/brokensystem2/index2.html.

original jurisdiction and the United States had 110, the ratio of death sentences to homicides was actually higher in Japan than in the United States. By measures such as these, Japan is not "careful" in its use of capital punishment. It is a vigorous killing state, on par with some of the most aggressive death penalty states in America.[7]

Death Is Not Different in Japan

Japanese officials claim to administer capital punishment carefully and cautiously, but reality contradicts their claims. For starters, Japanese law makes no promise of super due process. More specifically, there are at least 12 ways in which death is *not* different in Japan.[8] The net result is a legal system that is careless about capital punishment.

- 1. No Advance Notice About Whether a Case Is Capital: Japanese prosecutors make no advance announcement as to whether they will seek a sentence of death. The disclosure is only made on the penultimate day of trial, after all the evidence has been presented and just before the defense makes its closing argument. This non-disclosure policy makes it difficult for Japanese bar associations to provide institutional support of the kind that many American capital defenders take for granted. The non-disclosure policy also means that while Japan has a system of capital punishment, it does not really

---

[7] David T. Johnson, "American Capital Punishment in Comparative Perspective", *Law & Social Inquiry*, Vol. 36, No. 4 (Fall 2011), p. 1052.

[8] David T. Johnson, "Progress and Problems in Japanese Capital Punishment", in Roger Hood and Surya Deva, editors, *Confronting Capital Punishment in Asia: Human Rights, Politics, and Public Opinion* (Oxford University Press, 2013), pp. 175–180. In addition to the 12 problems summarized in the text, Japan has not signed several international treaties related to capital punishment, including the Second Optional Protocol to the International Covenant on Civil and Political Rights, which was created by the United Nations in 1989 and has been ratified by more than 70 nations, and it has not established the punishment of life without parole. All American states that retain capital punishment provide for the penalty of life without parole, as do America's federal and military justice systems. Life without parole would give judges and lay judges in Japan a harsh sentencing option between life with the possibility of parole and the penalty of death. Its availability in America is one reason why death sentences and executions have dropped sharply since 2000.

have "capital trials" because, until a trial ends, nobody but the prosecutors know whether the defendant's life is at stake.⁹
- **2. No Separate Stage for Sentencing**: Capital trials in Japan are not bifurcated into separate guilt and sentencing phases, even when the defendant denies guilt, as defendant Ino Kazuo did in a murder trial in Tokyo in 2011. Ino was ultimately sentenced to death by a lay judge panel that learned almost nothing about what kind of person the 60-year-old defendant was, or what kind of life he had lived. For a system that purports to value "precise" decision-making (*seimitsu shiho*) as one foundation for its criminal process, this is a peculiar way to make judgments about life and death. In the murder trial of Tateyama Tatsumi in Chiba, the Chief Judge did not even allow an expert witness to appear for the defense to testify about one of the central issues in the trial: whether Tateyama has a cognitive and developmental disorder. The Chief Judge ruled in the pretrial process that such testimony would confuse the lay judges.
- **3. Victims' Demands for Punishment Distort Fact-Finding**: Since capital trials are not bifurcated in Japan, victims and survivors are allowed *during the fact-finding procedure* to make statements about what punishment they want. This is a dangerous practice for two reasons: because research shows that courts are more likely to convict defendants if they are permitted to hear punitive sentencing requests, and because victims' wishes about punishment are supposed to be irrelevant with respect to the question of guilt. There is no principled way to justify this practice, and in fact the Code of Criminal Procedure gives judges ample discretion to prevent it from happening. Yet Japanese judges routinely allow it to occur. The Victim Participation System, which expands the rights and amplifies the voices of victims and survivors, also raises the risk that emotional demands for harsh punishment will distort truth-finding at trial (see Chapter 5).¹⁰ In the murder trial of Ino Kazuo in Tokyo, the victim's bereaved son was

---

⁹ David T. Johnson, "Capital Punishment without Capital Trials in Japan's Lay Judge System", *The Asia-Pacific Journal/Japan Focus*, Vol. 7 (March 16, 2009), pp. 1–40, at https://apjjf.org/-David-T.-Johnson/3461/article.html.

¹⁰ David T. Johnson, "Does Capital Punishment Bring Closure to Victims?", in Ivan Simonovic, editor, *Death Penalty and the Victims* (United Nations, 2016), pp. 75–82.

permitted to state that he wanted the defendant sentenced to death—and this was on the second day of trial, when fact-finding had barely begun. In the murder trial of Tateyama Tatsumi in Chiba, two surviving parents, their attorney, four victims, and two prosecutors—9 people in all—spent 195 minutes in the final trial session demanding that Tateyama be sentenced to death. The allotted time for the defense's closing argument was 60 minutes.

- 4. Simple Scripts and Rough Justice: The lay judge system which took effect in 2009 has reduced the importance of "precision" (*seimitsusa*) in Japan's criminal process, and this is especially conspicuous in capital trials. Before 2009, capital trials lasted for many months or years; trial sessions were held discontinuously, with one every few weeks or months, which gave all of the parties time to examine issues repeatedly while the trial inched toward the finish line. There were costs to that method of course—justice delayed can be justice denied, and some judges were transferred in mid-trial—but whatever its flaws, the previous system could not be accused of being insufficiently deliberate. In contrast, many capital trials in the lay judge system follow simple scripts, and many judges insist that trials stay "on schedule." This stress on efficiency may satisfy a Supreme Court that has instructed judges to finish lay judge trials efficiently, but surely concerns about convenience should not trump the imperative to administer capital punishment carefully.[11]

- 5. Vague Sentencing Standards: The "*Nagayama* standards" enumerated by Japan's Supreme Court in 1983 provide little guidance to the judges and lay judges who make life-and-death decisions. Many lay judges have noted this in post-trial press conferences, and many legal professionals regard the nine *Nagayama* factors as little more than a list of talking points for courts to consider. The *Nagayama* precedent also provides no direction about how to weigh the various factors, leaving life-and-death decision-making largely ungoverned by rules of law.[12]

---

[11] David T. Johnson, "Capital Punishment without Capital Trials in Japan's Lay Judge System", *The Asia-Pacific Journal/Japan Focus*, Vol. 7 (March 16, 2009), pp. 1–40, at https://apjjf.org/-David-T.-Johnson/3461/article.html.

[12] See, for example, Horikawa Keiko, *Shikei no Kijun: 'Nagayama Saiban' ga Nokoshita Mono* (Nihon Hyoronsha, 2009); and Nagata Kenji, *Shikei Sentaku Kijun no Kenkyu* (Kansai Daigaku Shuppanbu, 2010).

- **6. No Automatic Review**: In Japan, there is no automatic appellate review for defendants who have been sentenced to death. In recent years, about one-third of all death sentences have been finalized without review by the Supreme Court. Most of these involve condemned inmates who have abandoned their appeals.[13] This is not only careless, it also injects an element of arbitrariness in life-and-death decision-making. Are people who volunteer to be executed somehow more deserving of death than those who insist on their own innocence? Moreover, half or more of death row inmates in Japan file requests for retrial in order to avoid execution, but these requests have no legal effect on the Minister of Justice's authority to order a hanging, and some condemned inmates are hanged despite a pending petition. The lack of mandatory review in Japan increases the risk of executing the innocent or the undeserving. This risk is magnified because no inmate on death row has received executive clemency in Japan since Ishii Kenjiro had his death sentence commuted to life imprisonment in 1975. Unlike Thailand, Malaysia, Indonesia, and other death penalty countries in Asia, executive clemency in capital cases in Japan is all but dead.[14]
- **7. No Special Procedures for Selecting Lay Judges**: In Japan, there are no special procedures for selecting lay judges to serve in murder trials. The defense and the prosecution each receive several rights to challenge prospective lay judges, but their use in the pretrial process is little more than a guessing game because the parties receive almost no information about the citizens who have been called to serve, and because the parties are not allowed to ask meaningful questions about the lay judge candidates during the selection procedure. Moreover, some lay judges are replaced while a trial is in session. In the capital trial of Ino Kazuo, a lay judge who asked many questions to the witnesses during trial was replaced

---

[13] The Death Penalty Project in association with the Centre for Prisoners' Rights, *The Death Penalty in Japan* (London: The Death Penalty Project, 2013), p. 27. By comparison, in recent years about 11 percent of death-sentenced prisoners in the United States hastened their own executions by abandoning their appeals. See Meredith Martin Rountree, "'I'll Make Them Shoot Me': Accounts of Death Row Prisoners Advocating for Execution", *Law & Society Review*, Vol. 46, No. 3 (September 2012), pp. 589–622.

[14] Daniel Pascoe, *Last Chance for Life: Clemency in Southeast Asian Death Penalty Cases* (Oxford University Press, 2019).

during the deliberations that followed the final trial session, but the Chief Judge did not take the trouble to inform the parties about the change, and the defense only discovered it after Ino was sentenced to death. In the capital trial of Tateyama Tatsumi, one lay judge slept repeatedly during the first eight trial sessions. Defense lawyers asked the Chief Judge to address this fundamental issue of fairness, but the Chief Judge (who also dozed during trial) refused to act until the day before the final trial session, when his hand was forced by a written petition from the defense that was supported by statements from several persons who were watching the trial with dismay over how much the lay judge slumbered during a murder trial. An American federal court judge (Reggie Walton) who warned jurors to stay awake during a trial said "I don't think God has given us a supernatural ability to sleep and listen at the same time." Some Japanese judges apparently have a different view.[15]

- 8. <u>Law Is Not Explained in Open Court</u>: In Japan, the presiding judge instructs (*setsuji*) lay judges about the law in the privacy of the deliberation room, not in open court where the prosecution, the defense, and trial watchers can assess these important directives. There is reason to worry that some judges present a pro-prosecution—and pro-death penalty—version of the law to lay judges. The failure to instruct lay judges in open court may also violate the defendant's Constitutional right to a public trial. In August 2010, a well-known defense lawyer (Takano Takashi) who was offering a training course in trial advocacy happened to eat lunch in a deliberation room used by Osaka District Court Chief

---

[15] Here is one passage from my own letter to the Chief Judge in Tateyama's trial, which the defense included in its petition to the court: "On the afternoon of June 14, I decided to count how many times Lay Judge 2 slept. From 1:15 to 1:45 PM, he fell asleep at least 33 times. Yes, that's right: 33 times in 30 minutes. Lay Judge 2 was sleeping almost constantly during this period of time (and at other times as well). I could have kept track for a longer period but, frankly, watching people sleep is not very interesting, so I stopped watching and counting at 1:45 PM. If Lay Judge 2 had been driving a car, he would have crashed." At the end of this letter I told the Chief Judge that "I also have noticed you sleeping during this trial, but because your sleeping is not as obvious or as frequent as that of Lay Judge 2, I will not request that you recuse yourself… But I do think it is a good idea for you to stay awake during murder trials. Do you agree with my view?" The Chief Judge did not reply to my letter.

Judge Higuchi Hiroaki and his colleagues. On entering the room, Takano was initially pleased to see that "Rules for Criminal Trials" had been posted on a whiteboard, presumably to instruct lay judges who are amateurs in the law. But the more closely Takano read the rules, the more concerned he became. Incredibly, the whiteboard presented guidelines for convicting defendants but omitted language about when it is appropriate to acquit. In Takano's words, "I was amazed. I trembled a little. And I was indignant. *You mean they'll even do shit like this?!* This is what I cried out in my heart. If judges feel like it, they can use clever methods in the secrecy of the deliberation room to lead lay judges to their preferred conclusion without anyone noticing."[16]

- 9. Death by Majority: In Japan, there is no requirement that all judges and lay judges agree that a death sentence is deserved, nor is there a requirement that a "super-majority" of seven or eight of the nine people on the panel agree before the ultimate penalty is imposed. A "mixed majority"—five votes, with at least one from a professional judge—is enough to condemn a person to death. This decision rule is hardly "cautious" about capital punishment. In all American jurisdictions that retain capital punishment, a death sentence can only be imposed if all 12 jurors agree that death is the appropriate sanction.
- 10. Passive Defense Lawyers: The assumption that death is not different also influences Japanese defense lawyers, mainly by inhibiting them from aggressively challenging the state's case for death. In some of the capital trials I have watched, defense lawyers were strikingly passive about contesting the state's case against the defendant, and they also were reluctant to directly challenge the propriety of capital punishment.[17] Even more striking is the fact that for the past half-century, Japanese lawyers have almost never

---

[16] Quoted in David T. Johnson, "War in a Season of Slow Revolution: Defense Lawyers and Lay Judges in Japanese Criminal Justice", *Asia-Pacific Journal/Japan Focus*, Vol. 9 (June 29, 2011), pp. 1–11.

[17] David T. Johnson, "War in a Season of Slow Revolution: Defense Lawyers and Lay Judges in Japanese Criminal Justice", *Asia-Pacific Journal/Japan Focus*, Vol. 9 (June 29, 2011), pp. 1–11.

challenged the constitutionality of capital punishment in general or hanging in particular.[18] There are several reasons for this passivity, including the fact that Japan's Supreme Court has long been conservative. But in comparative perspective, the reluctance of Japanese lawyers to raise legal challenges that are routinely made in American jurisdictions seems to reflect tacit acceptance of the legitimacy of capital punishment. Until recently, Japanese defense lawyers rarely presented detailed evidence about the defendant's life history. Such presentations are often made in the sentencing stage of American capital trials. One key cause of the dramatic decline in American death sentences has been the ardent efforts of "mitigation specialists," who thoroughly investigate a capital defendant's "life story" and then tell it in detail to the jurors who decide whether to condemn the defendant to death. Japan has more than 30,000 lawyers but not a single mitigation specialist. The guidelines for paying state-appointed attorneys (*kokusen bengonin*), who do the bulk of criminal defense work in Japan, create little incentive to expend the arduous effort that is needed to construct a persuasive account of a defendant's life. The senior defense lawyer for Tateyama Tatsumi was paid no more for his work in that case than he was paid for work in other criminal cases where the stakes were much lower. That defense lawyer asked for a more appropriate fee, but his request was rejected by the court because there is no rule about capital cases in the fee guidelines. In this economic sense too, death is not different in Japan.

- 11. Prosecutors Can Appeal Non-death Decisions: In Japan, prosecutors are allowed two bites of the death penalty apple. If a District Court does not impose the ultimate penalty, prosecutors can ask an appellate court to reverse the original decision. This is what occurred in the case of a juvenile who was sentenced to death by the Hiroshima High Court in 2008 for killing a mother and her infant daughter in Hikari City nine years earlier.[19] The right of

---

[18] As explained in Chapter 3, there is one significant exception: the murder trial of Takami Sunao in 2011, in which Japanese defense lawyers raised the issue of whether hanging is unconstitutionally cruel. In this case, the Osaka District Court held that hanging is constitutional.

[19] Masuda Michiko, *Fukuda kun o Koroshite Nani ni Naru: Hikari-shi Boshi Satsugai Jiken no Kansei* (Tokyo: Inshidentsu, 2009).

prosecutors to appeal non-death sentences serves the value of consistency by allowing appellate courts to check whether like cases are being treated alike, but criminal trials at the appellate level tend to be far faster and rougher than the first-instance trials where oral testimony is heard. Here, too, one sees evidence of the assumption that capital cases do not require special procedures or protections.
- 12. Secrecy and Democracy: As will be explained in more detail in the next chapter, the administration of hanging in Japan is surrounded by secrecy and silence to an extent seldom seen in other death penalty nations. The main function of Japan's policy of secrecy is to protect the system of capital punishment—including the premise that death is not different—from outside scrutiny and criticism. There is also a problem of secrecy related to lay judges, who by law are not permitted to disclose "confidential" information about their experiences at trial. This coerced silence prevents the public from knowing and talking about how life-and-death decisions are made. The secrecy and silence that surround Japanese capital punishment belie official claims that it is administered in a manner that is cautious and careful.

Two Ways Law Can Fail

In the years leading up to the start of Japan's lay judge system in 2009, more than 500 "mock trials" were held. The main objective was to anticipate the problems that might occur in the new trial system and to prepare for the complexities that inevitably accompany fundamental reforms of this kind. Despite this seemingly meticulous preparation, not a single mock trial was held in which prosecutors sought a sentence of death and a tribunal was asked to make a life-or-death decision. Here again is evidence of the assumption that death is not a different form of punishment in Japan.

The assumption that there is nothing special about capital cases is manifest at every level of Japanese adjudication, including the Supreme Court. I once asked a veteran journalist (Yamaguchi Susumu, the co-author of a fine book[20] on Japan's Supreme Court) whether the

---

[20] Yamaguchi Susumu and Miyaji Yu, *Saikosai no Anto: Shosuiken ga Jidai o Kirihiraku* (Asahi, 2011).

country's highest court considers death a "different" (*tokubetsu*) form of punishment. He said "yes," but when I asked *how* death is deemed different by the Supreme Court, he offered two replies, neither of which provides meaningful support for the assertion that the country's top court regards death as a special form of punishment. His first point was that before deciding whether to finalize (*kakutei*) a sentence of death, the Supreme Court gives defense lawyers an opportunity to make an oral argument—a privilege rarely granted to defense lawyers in other criminal cases. When I asked whether these oral arguments are little more than "empty rituals" (as many defense lawyers assert), Yamaguchi conceded that they are largely ceremonial, and that they seldom have a significant effect on the Justices' thinking. The second part of his answer was that the Justices on Japan's Supreme Court read the relevant documents "carefully" in capital cases. This response is revealing in two ways. For one thing, it suggests that Justices might *not* read records carefully in other kinds of cases. For another, trusting Justices to read the record "carefully" assumes there is no need for special procedures and protections in capital cases—much less for "super due process." I have studied criminal justice in Japan for the past thirty years, and I see no good reason to trust Justices on the Supreme Court (or any other judges) in this way. Like other scholars of Japanese criminal justice, I see many reasons to worry that judges will continue to defer to the prosecution, as they have done for decades.[21]

What happens to Supreme Court Justices in the United States and Japan as the result of hearing capital appeals? In a decision by the U.S. Supreme Court in 1972 (*Furman v. Georgia*), Justice Thurgood Marshall famously observed that if the American people were better informed about the reality of capital punishment, they would find it "shocking, unjust, and unacceptable." His hunch, which came to be known as the "Marshall hypothesis," has been the subject of much study, and its clearest confirmation comes from the death penalty conversions that many Justices have experienced while sitting on the U.S. Supreme

---

[21] See, for example, Hirano Ryuichi, "Diagnosis of the Current Code of Criminal Procedure", *Law in Japan*, Vol. 22 (1989), pp. 129–142; and Daniel H. Foote, "Policymaking by the Japanese Judiciary in the Criminal Justice Field," *Hoshakaigaku*, No. 72 (2010), pp. 6–45.

Court.²² For example, in 1976 America's highest Court held (in *Gregg v. Georgia*) by a 7 to 2 majority that the new capital statutes enacted by states after the *Furman* decision had found capital punishment unconstitutional (because its arbitrary administration was like "being struck by lightning") were now constitutional. The *Gregg* decision restarted the American machinery of capital punishment that had been stopped by *Furman* four years before, and three of the seven votes in the majority were cast by Justices Powell, Stevens, and Stewart. By the end of their tenures on the bench—after many years of confronting the kinds of "capital error" described earlier in this chapter—these three Justices had come to conclude that it is impossible to administer the death penalty in a manner that is fair, just, and accurate. Their knowledge of the actual practice of capital punishment had converted them into opponents of the sanction.²³

One leading scholar of American capital punishment has said that the actual practice of capital punishment in America is so inconsistent with the country's core legal values that "if you love the law, you must hate the death penalty."²⁴ Similarly, in 2009, the American Law Institute, the most prestigious law reform organization in the United States, withdrew its approval for the death penalty standards it had created in the Model Penal Code of 1963 because those standards had failed to provide adequate guidance for the juries who must decide which defendants should die. As another scholar observed,

> Now that the creators of the modern system of death penalty sentencing have disowned that system, there is no support for distinguishing the current death penalty lottery from the lawless system that *Furman* condemned [in 1972]. The apparatus that the Supreme Court rushed to embrace in [the *Gregg* decision of] 1976 has been exposed as a conspicuous failure.²⁵

---

²² Carol S. Steiker, "The Marshall Hypothesis Revisited", *Howard Law Journal*, Vol. 52, No. 3 (2009), pp. 522ff.

²³ Evan J. Mandery, *A Wild Justice: The Death and Resurrection of Capital Punishment in America* (W. W. Norton, 2013), pp. 432–440.

²⁴ Austin Sarat, *When the State Kills: Capital Punishment and the American Condition* (Princeton University Press, 2001), p. 253.

²⁵ Franklin E. Zimring, "Pulling the Plug on Capital Punishment", *The National Law Journal* (December 7, 2009).

In sum, here is the conclusion about capital punishment in the United States: lots of legal promises to administer the ultimate penalty fairly, justly, and accurately—and broken promises galore. Yet law can fail in more than one way. If the law of capital punishment in America fails to fulfill many of its promises, law in Japan fails by refusing to make many promises at all. This can be called a failure of aspiration and political will.[26] The low ideals Japan has established for the administration of capital punishment help explain why Justices on its Supreme Court (unlike Justices on the U.S. Supreme Court) do not change their mind about this issue. When there are few requirements to satisfy before imposing a sentence of death, there is little room for frustration or failure, and there is no need to change one's mind.[27]

In the years to come, Japan could reform its approach to capital punishment in two ways. On the one hand, the courts and the country could start to take seriously the assertion its Supreme Court made seven decades ago—that "a single life weighs more than the entire earth." This road to reform would require significant changes in the Code of Criminal Procedure, but an even more fundamental requirement would be greater fidelity to existing law on the part of Japanese judges. At the top of my own list of necessary reforms are the introduction of a separate stage for sentencing in capital cases, and a decision rule requiring more than a mere majority in order to condemn a person to death.

In the second path to reform, Japan would renounce capital punishment on the grounds that it is impossible to administer it in a manner that is fair, just, and accurate. America has tried much harder than Japan to construct such a death penalty system, and the most reasonable conclusion to reach is that it has failed, badly. As U.S. Supreme Court Justice Harry Blackmun concluded in 1994,

---

[26] David T. Johnson, "The Death Penalty in Japan: Secrecy, Silence, and Salience", in Austin Sarat and Christian Boulanger, editors, *The Cultural Lives of Capital Punishment: Comparative Perspectives* (Stanford University Press, 2005), pp. 261–264.

[27] The other reason there are so many death penalty "conversions" among Justices on the U.S. Supreme Court and so few in Japan is that American Justices serve an average of 26 years, compared with just 6 years for Justices in Japan. The longer term of service means that American Justices encounter more capital cases and more capital error. See Andrew Cohen, "Why Don't [U.S.] Supreme Court Justices Ever Change Their Minds in *Favor* of the Death Penalty", *The Atlantic*, December 2013.

> From this day forward, I no longer shall tinker with the machinery of death. For more than 20 years I have endeavored…to develop…rules that would lend more than the mere appearance of fairness to the death penalty endeavor…Rather than continue to coddle the court's delusion that the desired level of fairness has been achieved…I feel…obligated simply to concede that the death penalty experiment has failed. It is virtually self-evident to me now that no combination of procedural rules or substantive regulations ever can save the death penalty from its inherent constitutional deficiencies… [T]his court eventually will conclude that the effort to eliminate arbitrariness while preserving fairness in the infliction of [death] is so plainly doomed to failure that it and the death penalty must be abandoned altogether…I may not live to see that day, but I have faith that eventually it will arrive.[28]

If Japan spends as long as America—almost half a century—trying to construct its own system of "super due process," I suppose the outcome could be a little less disappointing than Blackmun's lament suggests. Perhaps, but I doubt it. Comparative research should stretch our minds about what is possible and impossible. America's long experiment with capital punishment suggests that it may well be impossible to construct a system of capital justice that reaches only the rare right cases without also occasionally condemning the innocent or the undeserving.[29] In my view, this is the pivotal issue in every country that still has capital punishment, and Japan would be foolish to ignore the abundant evidence from the United States. Whatever road Japan chooses to travel in the future, one thing is clear: the present presumption that death is not different is deeply problematic. It may turn out that Japan can do little better at administering capital punishment than it is doing now. But if the country continues to employ capital punishment, surely it should try.

---

[28] *Callins v Collins* 510 US 1141 (1994).
[29] Scott Turow, *Ultimate Punishment: A Lawyer's Reflections on Dealing with the Death Penalty* (Farrar, Straus and Giroux, 2003), p. 114.

Open Access This chapter is licensed under the terms of the Creative Commons Attribution-NonCommercial-NoDerivatives 4.0 International License (http://creativecommons.org/licenses/by-nc-nd/4.0/), which permits any noncommercial use, sharing, distribution and reproduction in any medium or format, as long as you give appropriate credit to the original author(s) and the source, provide a link to the Creative Commons license and indicate if you modified the licensed material. You do not have permission under this license to share adapted material derived from this chapter or parts of it.

The images or other third party material in this chapter are included in the chapter's Creative Commons license, unless indicated otherwise in a credit line to the material. If material is not included in the chapter's Creative Commons license and your intended use is not permitted by statutory regulation or exceeds the permitted use, you will need to obtain permission directly from the copyright holder.

CHAPTER 3

When the State Kills in Secret

Abstract The secrecy that surrounds executions in Japan is taken to extremes seldom seen in other nations. To describe the reality of hanging in Japan (its sole method of execution since 1882), this chapter discusses two sources of evidence. First it summarizes recently discovered documents from the American Occupation of Japan (1945–1952), which reveal facts about hanging that have long been obscured by the country's secrecy policy. Then it describes a capital trial that occurred in Osaka in 2011, where the defense directly challenged the constitutionality of hanging for the first time since Japan's Supreme Court declared this method "constitutional" in 1955. These sources of information raise a question about execution that is hard to answer in the affirmative: Is it possible to hang a human being humanely?

Keywords Execution · Hanging · Secrecy · Silence · Occupation of Japan · Trial of Takami Sunao

In Japan and many other countries, executions used to be staged in public so that rulers could communicate to their subjects the political and cosmic forces at work when doing justice. Today, by contrast, executions are often represented as nonevents in which power is made minimally visible.¹ In most nations that continue to carry out executions, officials try to do so silently and invisibly, though there are large differences in the degree to which this aim is achieved. In Japan, the secrecy and silence that surround capital punishment are taken to extremes not seen in other nations.² The secrecy "gap" between Japan and the United States has narrowed in recent years, as American death penalty states have become increasingly clandestine in response to concerns about their lethal injection protocols and practices, but in many respects Japan remains an outlier with respect to openness.³ Consider the following features of capital punishment in Japan—the state that kills in secret.

- Inmates on death row are not notified of the date or time of execution until an hour or two before it occurs, and some may be given no notice at all. One former prison official has said that certain condemned inmates are extracted from their cells on the ruse that they are "wanted in the office."⁴ This sudden "your-time-has-come" policy has been called a "surprise attack" (*damashi-uchi*). Many death row inmates live for years or decades in high anxiety, wondering whether the present day will be their last. Menda Sakae, who was exonerated and released in 1983 after spending 34 years on death row, had this to say about Japan's prior notification policy: "Between 8:00 and 8:30 in the morning was the most critical time, because that was generally when prisoners were notified of their execution... You begin to feel the most terrible anxiety, because you don't know if they are going to stop in front of your cell. It is impossible to express how awful a feeling this was. I would have shivers down my spine. It was absolutely unbearable."⁵

---

¹ David Garland, *Peculiar Institution: America's Death Penalty in an Age of Abolition* (The Belknap Press of Harvard University Press, 2010), p. 52.

² David T. Johnson, "The Death Penalty in Japan: Secrecy, Silence, and Salience", in Austin Sarat and Christian Boulanger, editors, *The Cultural Lives of Capital Punishment: Comparative Perspectives* (Stanford University Press, 2005), pp. 251–273.

³ Robin Konrad, "Behind the Curtain: Secrecy and the Death Penalty in the United States" (Death Penalty Information Center, 2018), pp. 1–85, at https://files.deathpenalty-info.org/documents/pdf/SecrecyReport-2.f1560295685.pdf.

⁴ Sakamoto Toshio, *Shikei wa Ika ni Shikko Sareru ka* (Nihon Bungeisha, 2003), p. 69.

⁵ Menda Sakae, *Menda Sakae Gokuchu Noto: Watakushi no Miokutta Shikeishu-tachi* (Impakuto, 2004).

- Relatives of the condemned are told of the execution after the fact—as are defense lawyers, the media, and everyone else in Japanese society except for a handful of state officials. This minimizes protest and limits debate.
- In some cases, members of the execution team are given little prior notification, partly out of concern that if told in advance they may not show up for work. Corrections guards who participate in an execution receive extra pay of 20,000 yen ($180). Sakamoto Toshio, a former guard who witnessed hangings, has described the execution process as "unbearable." "It's awful," he recalls. "The body bounces like a 70 kilogram object on a nylon rope…There is no worse job." Guards on the execution team receive no counseling and, according to Sakamoto, are expected to "digest" the execution themselves.[6]
- No outsiders are permitted to attend hangings: no journalists, no relatives or friends of the victim or the condemned, and no members of the general public. Research in the United States has revealed that approximately 3–5 percent of all executions are botched, leading to prolonged suffering by the condemned during the execution process.[7] The botch rate in Japan is unknown because those who would be willing to say do not know, for they are excluded from the execution scene.
- Scholars and reporters are denied access to many official death penalty documents. This discourages research and reporting about capital punishment.
- Citizens and members of the media are almost never allowed to view the gallows, even when it is not in use. In 2010, Japanese authorities did permit a few selected reporters to make one 30-minute visit to the glass-walled execution room in the Tokyo Detention Center.
- A "spiritual advisor" can attend a hanging, but condemned persons are not free to choose who it will be. Advisors are selected from a list of state-approved clergy, none of whom is openly abolitionist.

---

[6] Miwa Suzuki, "Cruel, Secretive and Politically Popular: Japan's Death Penalty", *Japan Times*, September 12, 2018.

[7] Austin Sarat, *Gruesome Spectacles: Botched Executions and America's Death Penalty* (Stanford University Press, 2014).

Activity deemed "political" will result in removal from the list.[8] Proscribed behavior includes actions that might cultivate hope in the condemned.
- Prosecutors in the Ministry of Justice select execution dates strategically, to minimize the possibility of protest and debate. Among other calculations, executions frequently occur when Parliament is in recess, often on a Thursday or Friday, near the end of the news week, when people are becoming preoccupied with weekend activities.
- The Ministry of Justice provides no explanation or justification for why certain death row inmates are selected for hanging while others are permitted to continue living. After the 13 Aum executions in July 2018, 110 inmates remained under a finalized sentence of death. By law, any of them could be chosen to die at any time, leading critics to contend that the officials who make execution decisions (mostly prosecutors) are "playing god." In most years, only a few death row inmates are chosen for execution, according to criteria that are not made public.
- Between imposition of a death sentence and execution, inmates on death row are socially extinguished through the state's severe restrictions on meetings and correspondence. The stated reason for this policy is to promote "stable feelings" (*shinjo no antei*) in inmates and thereby help them "prepare for death." But one function of killing socially before killing physically is the facilitation of "smooth" executions in which demoralized inmates do not resist.[9]

In recent years the administration of executions in Japan has taken a few steps toward transparency. The Ministry of Justice, which legally and practically decides who among Japan's inmates with a finalized sentence of death will be executed (and when), now makes a brief post-execution announcement stating the name of the person executed and describing the crimes for which he or she was hanged (until 1999, the government made no announcement at all). And as described

---

[8] Adam Lyons, *Karma and Punishment: Prison Chaplaincy in Japan* (Harvard University Asia Center Press, forthcoming).

[9] David T. Johnson, "Where the State Kills in Secret: Capital Punishment in Japan", *Punishment & Society*, Vol. 8, No. 3 (July 2006), pp. 251–285.

in Chapter 1, in 2010, then-Minister of Justice Chiba Keiko created a study group in her Ministry to discuss Japan's death penalty policy, occasionally in sessions that were open to selected members of the public (the study group ended with a whimper of irrelevance, not a bang of reform). Minister of Justice Chiba also opened the gallows in Tokyo to a small group of journalists, one of the seven places in the country where condemned inmates are hanged. In my view, allowing a few selected reporters to view the gallows when not in use is like sitting in the Tokyo Dome when no one is playing baseball, for it reveals little about how the activity of interest is actually performed.

Despite these modest changes, the wall of silence surrounding executions in Japan remains largely intact.[10] Figure 3.1 illustrates this "capital blackout" with a photograph of a document that the Ministry of Justice provided to a defense lawyer who used the Disclosure of Information Act to request information about what had transpired at several recent hangings. In other released documents, the lopsided ratio of white space to black resembles that shown here. This execution record (*shikei shikko shimatsusho*) provides the date of execution (2007), but it obscures almost everything else, including the name of the person who was hanged, the location of the hanging, the court that imposed the sentence of death, the persons who attended the hanging and their organizational affiliations, and (in the largest blacked out section) notes that may or may not have been taken about the execution process.

Japanese officials seldom explain the state's policy of secrecy as it relates to capital punishment. That, after all, would be inconsistent with the policy. But occasionally they do offer justifications. None is compelling. Sometimes officials say secrecy is in the condemned inmate's interest, but research shows that most inmates on Japan's death row want to know their execution day in advance, so that they can better prepare for death, and because it eliminates the "is today the day?" anxiety they wake up with every morning. Sometimes officials say secrecy is a Japanese tradition, but officials have consciously and strategically expanded the reach of secrecy in the postwar period. In reality, this "tradition" is a recent invention. Sometimes officials say secrecy is in the interest of the execution team, but this amounts to an admission that the state's policy

---

[10] David T. Johnson, "Japan's Secretive Death Penalty Policy: Contours, Origins, Justifications, and Meanings", *Asian-Pacific Law & Policy Journal*, Vol. 7, No. 2 (Summer 2006), pp. 62–124.

Fig. 3.1 Japanese Ministry of Justice execution record, 2007

別　紙

執行経過

Fig. 3.1 (continued)

Fig. 3.1 (continued)

of secrecy serves the state's interest in seeing that executions are done as impersonally, bureaucratically, and non-controversially as possible. These are not democratic values. And sometimes officials claim the American way of execution—including the last-minute appeals and the "Forgive!" and "Kill him!" demonstrations that often occur outside prison walls—is unseemly and unattractive. It is, but claiming "the USA is worse" does not mean the Japanese way—"your time has come!"—is alright. Indeed, this Japanese justification reminds me of what my mother used to say ("don't change the subject!") when I excused my own bad behavior by suggesting that my brother had done something worse. It is, in a word, irrelevant.[11]

The French philosopher Albert Camus observed that "Instead of saying that the death penalty is first of all necessary and then adding that it is better not to talk about it, it is essential to say what it really is and then say, whether, being what it is, it is to be considered as necessary."[12]

---

[11] David T. Johnson, "Where the State Kills in Secret: Capital Punishment in Japan", *Punishment & Society*, Vol. 8, No. 3 (July 2006), pp. 264–268.

[12] Albert Camus, "Reflections on the Guillotine", in *Resistance, Rebellion, and Death* (Vintage, 1960), p. 178.

State officials in Japan have long practiced a "better not to talk about it" strategy. The lay judge tribunals that started in 2009—3 professional judges and 6 lay persons who adjudicate guilt and determine sentence in serious criminal cases—means that ordinary citizens are now responsible for making life-and-death decisions in murder trials. As will be discussed in Chapter 5, with this responsibility there has been more public discussion about some death penalty issues. Most notably, questions about the propriety of capital punishment have received increased attention, and there has been a push for more information about the death penalty to be revealed by state officials—especially those in the Ministry of Justice who function as gatekeepers to the gallows—so that more meaningful discussions can occur about fundamental questions, such as whether the state should kill, and who, and how many.[13] In this context, the question of *how* Japan executes has received more attention in recent years.

This rest of this chapter presents two sources of evidence to describe how the reality of hanging (Japan's sole method of execution since 1882) is depicted and discussed. It first summarizes recently discovered documents from the American Occupation (1945–1952) that reveal realities about hanging that long have been obscured by Japan's secrecy policy. It then describes a capital trial that occurred in Osaka in 2011, where the defense directly challenged the constitutionality of hanging for the first time since Japan's Supreme Court declared this method "constitutional" in 1955. These sources of information raise a question for the fifteen Justices and thirty-some research clerks on Japan's Supreme Court, and for the large majority of Japanese citizens who say they support capital punishment.[14] Is it possible to execute a human being humanely?

---

[13] See, for example, Taguchi Masayoshi, editor, *Saibanin no Atama no Naka: 14nin no Hajimete Monogatari* (Gendai Jinbunsha, 2013); and Fukui Atsushi, editor, *Shikei to Mukiau Saibanin no Tame ni* (Gendaijinbunsha, 2011).

[14] In recent public opinion polls, approximately 80 percent of Japanese adults have said that the death penalty is "unavoidable." As will be discussed in Chapter 6, the survey questions that elicit these answers are worded and framed in problematic ways. See Mai Sato, *The Death Penalty in Japan: Will the Public Tolerate Abolition?* (Springer VS, 2014).

Occupation Truths

States that practice capital punishment have a legitimation challenge: They need to distinguish how their killing differs from the criminal killing they aim to condemn.[15] In the United States, one major legitimation strategy has been the effort to kill more "softly" and "humanely." This approach—to give the condemned a "kinder and gentler" death—helps explain the frequent changes in execution method that America has experienced over the last century or so—from hanging to electrocution to the gas chamber to lethal injection. The American quest to kill without imposing more pain than "necessary" is not so much about sparing the condemned from suffering as it is about convincing the administrators and spectators of death that capital punishment is "civilized."[16]

The Japanese state faces a similar legitimacy challenge but answers the call quite differently. There have been no significant changes in execution method in Japan since 1873, when a new gallows was introduced after an old-fashioned hanging was botched. Today, hanging remains the only method in each of Japan's seven execution centers, and since a Supreme Court opinion in 1955 upholding the constitutionality of hanging, there has been little discussion of alternative methods of execution. The lack of debate is not because the Japanese way of hanging is humane. In Japan as in India, Pakistan, Singapore, Malaysia, Iran, and Iraq, the point of hanging is to cut or crush the spinal cord by tearing it from the brain stem. If the initial shock of the drop is not fatal, death is completed by strangulation.[17]

Some hangings are botched in Japan, as they are in other countries. A former prosecutor once told me that a prison official told him that following one bungled hanging, a member of the execution team finished the job with a judo hold. But the secrecy surrounding capital

---

[15] Austin Sarat, *When the State Kills: Capital Punishment and the American Condition* (Princeton University Press, 2001), p. 21.

[16] David Garland, *Peculiar Institution: America's Death Penalty in an Age of Abolition* (The Belknap Press of Harvard University Press, 2010), pp. 268–272.

[17] Nakagawa Tomomasa Bengodan and Walter Rabl, editors, *Koshukei wa Zangyaku na Keibatsu de wa Nai no ka? Shimbun to Hoigaku ga Kataru Shinjitsu* (Gendaijinbunsha, 2011).

punishment in Japan helps explain the absence of controversy over execution methods. In effect, "killing secretly" instead of "killing softly" has been the Japanese state's legitimation strategy. If one meaning of lethal injection in the United States is that state killing is different than ordinary murder because it is done humanely, the message conveyed in Japan has long been that state killing is state business.

The U.S. Occupation (1945–1952) bequeathed two death penalty legacies to Japan. The first is the retention of capital punishment. As explained in Chapter 1, Occupation authorities could have abolished capital punishment in Japan as they did in Germany after World War II, but they elected not to, in large part because they were determined to put "war criminals" to death in the Tokyo War Crimes Trial.[18] The second Occupation legacy is a policy of "censored democracy" which has fostered a political consciousness of passive acquiescence to the silences dictated by Japan's death penalty secrecy.[19] Viewed historically, Japan's policy of secrecy and silence is partly an American invention.

The documents discovered by Professor Nagata Kenji on microfiche in Japan's National Diet Library contain the records of 46 persons who were hanged between July 1948 and March 1951, a period during which Japan was occupied by the American military and ruled by General Headquarters (GHQ) and General Douglas MacArthur, the Supreme Commander for the Allied Powers (SCAP).[20] The documents include execution planning papers (*shikei shikko kiansho*), execution reports (*shikei shikko shimatsusho*), and letters. Most of the documents were composed by prison wardens or by chiefs of the Japanese detention facilities where executions occurred. They are significant because they provide a peak behind the veil that has shrouded Japanese hangings since the policy of secrecy was established in the 1960s and 1970s. The 46 hangings are a little less than 40 percent of all the hangings that occurred during this 33-month period. They may be unrepresentative in some respects, albeit in ways one cannot know because no records have been

---

[18] Richard H. Minear, *Victors' Justice: The Tokyo War Crimes Trial* (Charles E. Tuttle Company, 1971); and Yuma Totani, *The Tokyo War Crimes Trial: The Pursuit of Justice in the Wake of World War II* (Harvard University Asia Center, 2009).

[19] John Dower, *Embracing Defeat: Japan in the Wake of World War II* (W. W. Norton, 1999), Chapter 14.

[20] Nagata Kenji, *GHQ Bunsho ga Kataru Nihon no Shikei Shikko: Kobunsho kara Semaru Koshukei no Jittai* (Gendaijinbunsha, 2013).

discovered for the rest of the hangings carried out in this period. Still, the records that are available tell important truths about the age and social status of the condemned, their last words, and the duration of their executions.[21]

The Occupation records show that the age of the condemned at the time of execution has increased dramatically since the 1950s. In the Occupation sample, the median age at hanging was 27, with the youngest person hanged being 23 and the oldest 63. By contrast, in recent decades the median age at hanging was 56—more than double the median age in the Occupation. In the 20 years between 1993 and 2012, almost 40 percent of all persons executed were over 60 years of age. It appears Japan has one of the most geriatric death rows in the world, and there seem to be two main reasons for this graying of its gallows. First, Japan's homicide rate has dropped dramatically since the 1950s. The main proximate cause of the decline is a large decrease in the percentage of homicides committed by young men. As young killers have been vanishing, older killers have come to constitute a larger proportion of homicide offenders.[22] Second, in the 1940s and 1950s, executions in Japan were usually carried out within a few months of a finalized sentence of death. Today, by contrast, a sentence of death is often the prelude to a long appeals process. The secrecy that surrounds executions means little media attention gets focused on how senior citizens are hanged. On Christmas Day in 2006, for example, the two people hanged in Tokyo were ages 75 and 77, respectively. Neither could walk to the gallows on his own, and both were in the process of appealing for retrial at the time of execution. These facts passed almost unnoticed in the perfunctory media coverage that followed their executions.

The Occupation documents also provide evidence that in Japan as in other death penalty nations, persons who get executed tend to be poor and poorly connected. Seven of the 46 persons hanged were ethnically Korean (15 percent). Since Koreans constituted only about 3 percent of Japan's total population at the end of the Pacific War, they are "overrepresented" in this execution sample by a factor of 5. In some

---

[21] Kenji Nagata and David T. Johnson, "Hanging in Japan: What Occupation Era Documents and a Lay Judge Trial Teach About the State That Still Kills in Secret", *Punishment & Society*, Vol. 16, No. 3 (July 2014), pp. 227–257.

[22] David T. Johnson, "The Vanishing Killer: Japan's Postwar Homicide Decline", *Social Science Japan Journal*, Vol. 9, No. 1 (April 2006), pp. 73–90.

capital cases, SCAP officials wondered whether Japanese judges discriminated against Koreans in sentencing and therefore performed a special "Review of Sentences Imposed upon Koreans" after judicial appeals had been exhausted. More broadly, the Occupation records provide reason to believe there was capital bias against other have-nots, for nearly 70 percent of the persons in the Occupation records (31/46) were unemployed at the time they committed their capital offenses, and more than 30 percent (14/46) were homeless. These are far higher percentages than the percentages of people in the general population who were unemployed and/or homeless.

In the Occupation records, communications between the condemned and their family and friends varied from case to case. Eight of the 46 men in the GHQ/SCAP sample received no letters or visitors between the time their conviction was "finalized" (*kakutei*) and their execution, whereas a man who was hanged in 1950 received at least 14 visitors and 66 letters in the 11 months preceding his execution (he also sent 280 letters of his own). It appears there was substantially more freedom for death row inmates to communicate with outsiders in the 1940s and 1950s than there is today. The secrecy that surrounds executions in Japan deepened in the 1960s and 1970s in response to the rise of an abolitionist movement, out of concern that the emergence of "support groups" for inmates on death row would make administering death more difficult for corrections officials, and out of a desire to prevent suicide by inmates who had been notified that soon they would be hanged.[23]

In contrast to death rows in the United States, where the culture of capital punishment finds expression in "last words," "final meals," and other "farewell" expressions, little is known about what the men and women on Japan's death rows think and feel before their execution. But the Occupation documents do provide some insight into the Japanese past that can inform our musings about the present. In the Occupation, death row inmates' "final words" took four main forms. Some inmates expressed *thanks* to officials of the correctional institutions for treating them kindly. Some left *warnings* for family members, as did a man hanged in Nagoya in 1951, who said his child should avoid gambling offenses of the kind that led to his own capital offense (robbery-murder). Some offenders left *haiku* or *tanka* poems of the kind

---

[23] David T. Johnson, "Where the State Kills in Secret: Capital Punishment in Japan", *Punishment & Society*, Vol. 8, No. 3 (July 2006), pp. 261–264.

that have been composed by criminal offenders in Japan since the feudal period. A 33-year-old man hanged in Osaka in 1951 left the following forlorn poem:

> The spring wind
> Blew through the tree sprouts
> But did not blow to this place

The last form of "final words" was the most common. In the Occupation records, 43 of the 46 persons (93 percent) expressed *regret* for their crimes. Regret, remorse, and apology have long been central values in Japanese culture and in Japan's criminal court communities, but the extent of their presence in these Occupation documents is striking. The final words of the condemned were recorded by prison officials who may have omitted messages ("I am innocent") they did not like and who may have highlighted messages ("Thank you, and I am sorry") that were welcome, but the bias of the recorders probably cannot fully explain the widespread presence of regret in the final words of the condemned.[24]

Finally, the Occupation records enable us to make several observations about time and executions. For one thing, executions during the Occupation were less concentrated in time than they have been in recent years. In 1950, for example, hangings occurred on at least 21 different days during the year, resulting in a total of 31 executions. By comparison, in 2008, when Japan executed 15 persons—the largest number of executions the country had carried out since 1975—all of the hangings occurred on only five days. Moreover, 27 of the 46 persons in the Occupation records (almost 60 percent) were executed alone on the day of their demise. In recent years, executions in Japan have almost always involved two or more persons who get hanged on the same day—often at the same gallows. The increased "lumpiness" of executions appears to be designed to minimize the number of occasions when hangings could attract public and media attention.

Hangings in the Occupation, like hangings in subsequent decades, usually occurred in the morning. In the Occupation records, the execution start times ranged from 9:19 a.m. to 2:39 p.m., but 42 of the

---

[24] Kenji Nagata and David T. Johnson, "Hanging in Japan: What Occupation Era Documents and a Lay Judge Trial Teach About the State That Still Kills in Secret", *Punishment & Society*, Vol. 16, No. 3 (July 2014), pp. 236–240.

46 hangings occurred before noon, and the four that occurred in the afternoon all occurred in Osaka. Hangings in Japan tend to be scheduled for the morning in order to reduce stress on the execution team and minimize the possibility of leaks to the media. Members of Japanese execution teams are typically told of their job assignment the day before a hanging, they are ordered not to tell anyone about it, and they are expected not to refuse the assignment. In some cases, executioners are only told of their assignment on the morning a hanging occurs, apparently out of fear that if told in advance they might not show up for work.

The duration of hangings in the Occupation records ranged from 10 minutes and 55 seconds (in Miyagi in 1950) to 21 minutes (in Nagoya in 1951). Thus, the longest hanging was almost twice as long as the shortest. The average length of all 46 hangings, from the time of the "drop" to the time a doctor confirmed death, was 14 minutes and 15 seconds, with a median time of 14 minutes. In the United States, three criteria have been identified by courts to indicate whether an execution method provides "a death within constitutional limits": the death must be painless, it must be non-lingering, and it must be instantaneous. Conversely, a death that is painful, lingering, or not instantaneous raises questions about "cruel and unusual punishment" under the Eighth Amendment to the U.S. Constitution. It is difficult to discern whether Occupation executions were problematic in these ways, for the records are not exhaustive accounts of what transpired during executions, and they were written by state officials who may not have recorded certain problematic events. Some doctors may also have allowed inmates to hang for several minutes after all signs of life had disappeared before declaring the person dead. Still, the Occupation evidence is troubling, for all of the Japanese hangings exceed by at least a factor of five the "two minutes or less" American standard for a "non-lingering" death that has been used to assess executions, and the Japanese average is more than seven times longer than this American threshold.

Japan's method of hanging has changed little since the Meiji period, so there is little reason to believe that execution lengths have become significantly shorter in the two-thirds of a century since the Occupation ended. If hangings in Japan are like executions in jurisdictions where state killings are more transparent, then some surely have been "botched" because of problems with the length or placement of the rope, or with the depth of the drop, or with the physiology of the condemned (among other possibilities). Research in the United States finds that botched executions take place with regular frequency. If we assume that hangings in Japan have been carried out no more and no less smoothly than executions in America (where research reveals a "botch rate" of 2.7–4.5 percent), then 19–32 of the 713 persons hanged between January 1946 and July 2017 would have had their executions botched. That would be, on the average, one botched hanging every two or three years. If capital punishment in Japan is "normal" in this respect, then the issue of hanging could be litigated under Article 36 of the Constitution, which declares that "cruel punishments are absolutely forbidden."[25] The next section examines the only significant effort in recent years to challenge the constitutionality of hanging in Japan.

Hanging on Trial

On July 5, 2009, 41-year-old Takami Sunao set light to a bucket of gasoline he had poured on the floor of a pachinko parlor in the city of Osaka. The subsequent blaze killed five people and injured 10 more. By Takami's own account, his attack was motivated by anger over his life circumstances, including employment difficulties and financial debt, and by the desire to exact revenge on a woman he referred to as "Mihi," who had been making his life miserable—and who did not exist. Despite his delusions, Takami admitted that his mass murder was premeditated. Moreover, before, during, and after his trial, he frequently said that he would like to die and that he would accept a sentence of death.

In Japanese criminal justice, premeditated murder that leads to the loss of more than two lives usually results in a death sentence—and so it did in Takami's case when the Osaka District Court condemned him to death on October 31, 2011. But unlike many criminal trials in Japan, this one was more than a rubber stamp ratifying the outcome prosecutors sought. Takami's trial lasted 60 days, making it the longest lay judge trial in the country up until that point. Two main issues were contested at his trial. First, the defense team argued that Takami lacked criminal responsibility (*sekinin noryoku*) because he was schizophrenic, while prosecutors argued (and the court ultimately concluded) that the defendant was mentally competent at the time of the crimes even though

---

[25] Kenji Nagata and David T. Johnson, "Hanging in Japan: What Occupation Era Documents and a Lay Judge Trial Teach About the State That Still Kills in Secret", *Punishment & Society*, Vol. 16, No. 3 (July 2014), pp. 240–242.

he was delusional due to his frequent use of methamphetamines. Second, the defense argued that hanging violates the prohibition against "cruel punishments" in Article 36 of Japan's Constitution. The court ultimately rejected this argument too, but it did so in language that recognized some of the realities of hanging that have been hidden from the Japanese public for decades.

Defense lawyers in this case wondered about the wisdom of challenging hanging because they knew that if the court rejected their claims, the effect might be to bolster the legitimacy of capital punishment. In the United States, efforts to "humanize" methods of execution have entrenched the death penalty, making what remains of this institution more resistant to repeal.[26] But in a case that seemed like an evidentiary slam dunk for the prosecution (in addition to Takami's confession, there was surveillance video of him starting the fire), defense lawyers believed that challenging hanging was one of the few ways his life might be saved. They also felt dismayed over how thoroughly Japanese defense attorneys had acquiesced to the legality of capital punishment over the past half-century.

The jurisprudence of capital punishment in Japan is easily summarized because there is little of it. In 1948, the Supreme Court held that capital punishment is not necessarily a "cruel punishment" even though some methods of execution are, such as burning at the stake or boiling in a cauldron—methods that had been used in Japan before the Meiji oligarchs encountered Western sensibilities about criminal punishment in the last third of the nineteenth century and reformed them in order to appear more "civilized" to the outside world. The same decision declared that a method of execution such as hanging that is deemed "constitutional" at present could become a "cruel punishment" under Article 36 if social circumstances and human morality changed. In 1955, the Supreme Court reaffirmed this position when it found that, compared with other methods of execution then being used in the world (strangulation, beheading, shooting, the electric chair, and the gas chamber), hanging is not an especially "cruel punishment" under Article 36.[27]

---

[26] Hugo Adam Bedau, "An Abolitionist's Survey of the Death Penalty in America Today", in Hugo Adam Bedau and Paul Cassell, editors, *Debating the Death Penalty: Should America Have Capital Punishment? The Experts from Both Sides Make Their Case* (Oxford University Press, 2004), pp. 15–50.

[27] Petra Schmidt, *Capital Punishment in Japan* (Brill, 2002), pp. 90–100.

Between this opinion in 1955 and Takami's arson attack in 2009—more than half a century—the constitutionality of hanging was never litigated in Japan.[28] The presence of lay judges at Takami's trial created a new opportunity to challenge the legal legitimacy of a method that has disappeared in the United States.[29]

Takami's defense team persuaded the Chief Judge in Osaka to ask the Ministry of Justice for information about whether persons who had been hanged in the past were injured in the process, but the Ministry refused the request with an empty bureaucratic formula: "*kaito itashikanemasu*" ("we are unable to reply to your request"). An Austrian scientist named Walter Rabl did testify at trial about the research he had done following the autopsies of approximately 300 persons who had committed suicide by hanging. Rabl, the President of the Austrian Society of Forensic Medicine, agreed to testify because he "was shocked that in a modern civilized country like Japan judicial hanging...is accepted as a 'non-cruel' method of execution" and because "there are so many misunderstandings and factual errors concerning death caused by judicial hanging." Rabl said that "any method of execution is cruel and incompatible with the Hippocratic oath," and he concluded that "judicial hanging is especially cruel in two respects": because the consciousness of a hanged person lasts at least 5–8 seconds and sometimes as long as 2–3 minutes, with severe injury and pain the norm; and because the result of judicial hanging for any individual is not predictable. Botched hangings, including decapitation, which Rabl observed in 2 percent of the corpses he examined, can occur even when an execution is carried out "according to standards."[30]

Former prosecutor Tsuchimoto Takeshi also testified for the defense in Takami's trial. He had worked as a prosecutor for 30 years before

---

[28] Nakagawa Tomomasa Bengodan and Walter Rabl, editors, *Koshukei wa Zangyaku na Keibatsu de wa Nai no ka? Shimbun to Hoigaku ga Kataru Shinjitsu* (Gendaijinbunsha, 2011).

[29] Until recently, hanging was authorized in the United States in Delaware, New Hampshire, and Washington, but the state Supreme Courts in Delaware (2016) and Washington (2018) have declared their capital sentencing procedures unconstitutional and resentenced all death-row prisoners to life without parole, while New Hampshire's legislature abolished that state's death penalty in 2019. Hanging is not authorized in the U.S. federal and military death penalty systems.

[30] Kenji Nagata and David T. Johnson, "Hanging in Japan: What Occupation Era Documents and a Lay Judge Trial Teach About the State That Still Kills in Secret", *Punishment & Society*, Vol. 16, No. 3 (July 2014), pp. 242–247.

becoming a professor at Tsukuba University. After resigning from the procuracy, his conservative positions on crime control and criminal justice were frequently quoted in the media. But six months before Takami's trial, a book was published about Tsuchimoto's prosecution of a man who had committed murder in 1966 and who was executed in 1971 despite Tsuchimoto's requests that he be granted clemency.[31] Tsuchimoto did not believe the offender was actually innocent, but he had exchanged letters with the inmate while the latter was on death row, and he had come to believe in the possibility of the inmate's redemption and atonement. When Tsuchimoto spoke with Takami's defense lawyers before he testified at Takami's trial, the former prosecutor expressed ambivalence about appearing as an expert witness. He had serious concerns about the propriety of hanging as an execution method, but he also supported capital punishment in principle and feared that he would be seen as betraying his friends and former colleagues in the procuracy if he testified for the defense. As he anticipated, when Tsuchimoto agreed to testify following persistent requests from the defense, prosecutors claimed he was violating the obligation of secrecy under Japan's National Public Service Law. In the end, however, Tsuchimoto was permitted to testify, and this was his main message:

> The death penalty itself is not unconstitutional, but death by hanging violates Article 36 of the Constitution...It is a gruesome and cruel punishment that one cannot bear to look at directly...Following the sound of the footplate being removed, the rope cut into the death row inmate's neck, leaving the inmate hanging in midair. A medical officer and other officials checked for the inmate's pulse and other signs, then announced that the inmate had died...When I looked at the person, who just a few moments earlier was breathing and warm, having their hands and legs bound so they couldn't resist and then swinging [on the rope], I thought it was gruesome...[Hanging] may have been appropriate at the time [of the Supreme Court's 1955 decision], but today it would be rash to judge that it is appropriate.[32]

---

[31] Horikawa Keiko, *Sabakareta Inochi: Shikeishu kara Todoita Tegami* (Kodansha, 2011).

[32] *Mainichi Japan*, "Japan Court Deliberates Hanging's Unconstitutionality", October 11, 2011.

Several victims and survivors of Takami's crimes harshly rebuked his defense lawyers for having the temerity to challenge hanging for such a heinous offender. Ultimately, the Osaka District Court sentenced Takami to death by hanging. Three pages of its 27-page opinion addressed the method of execution, including these words:

> The death penalty inevitably inflicts mental and physical pains on the inmate and involves brutality to some extent. But since the Constitution allows the death penalty to be retained, it evidently considers these pains to be unavoidable and inevitable. Therefore, an execution method constitutes 'cruel punishment', which is prohibited by Article 36 of the Constitution, only when it is especially brutal among possible execution methods... Obviously it is not required that an execution method relieve the mental and physical pains of the inmate to the utmost extent and keep them to some minimum, as if execution is a medical treatment...A method of execution should be considered a 'cruel punishment' only in the limited case when it is so impersonal and inhuman that it shocks a person with ordinary emotions. Otherwise, what kind of execution method is adopted is a matter to be decided through the discretion of the legislature.[33]

The idea in the Court's opinion that came to stand for the whole is that an inmate who is hanged "naturally must endure some mental and physical suffering" (*kutsu wa tozen kanju subeki*). Yet this conception of so-called "forgivable cruelty" seems inconsistent with the absolutist language of Article 36 of the Constitution, which states that "cruel punishments are absolutely forbidden."

As for the citizens who served as lay judges at Takami's trial, two themes emerged from their comments at the post-sentencing press conference. First, the lay judges seemed resigned to the inevitability of "cruelty" in the hanging process. Humane execution may well be a practical impossibility, but this court diverged from some American jurisprudence by finding that it is not necessary to keep the mental and physical pains of an executed inmate "to some minimum." Second, the lay judges stressed that Japan needs to encourage deeper debate about its death

---

[33] See "A Judgment of the Osaka District Court, October 31, 2011", at The Law Office of Goto Sadato, http://sgotolaw.com/jd.html.

penalty, so that policy and practice better reflect "citizens' sensibilities" (*shimin kankaku*).[34]

In 2013 the Osaka High Court rejected Takami's appeal and upheld his death sentence and the constitutionality of hanging. It held that Takami's own conduct was "extremely cruel," and that "hanging cannot be called cruel because the duration of felt suffering by the condemned is brief." The High Court also echoed the lay judges when it encouraged Japan's Diet to promote public discussion of execution methods. It said "leaving hanging as it is for 140 years without legal change is certainly not a desirable legislative policy," and it noted that the current method of hanging is "inconsistent in many respects" with the execution ordinance (*fukoku*) that was promulgated in 1873. Former prosecutor Tsuchimoto called the High Court's decision "highly significant" because it exposed "the legislative branch's negligence in failing to discuss execution methods," but in 2016 the Supreme Court finalized Takami's death sentence without seriously engaging the issue of hanging.[35] As of this writing in July 2019, Takami is still alive, but he could be hanged any day. Except for a handful of government officials, no one will know until after it occurs.

PROBLEMS AND PARADOXES

The Osaka District Court's recognition that executions "unavoidably" involve some kind of cruelty is consistent with findings from American research which conclude that even a routine or "properly performed" execution can cause intense pain and lingering death, and which find that executions—no matter the method—are regularly botched. Japan's jejune jurisprudence of executions seems more candid about the "inevitability" of cruelty than American courts have been, but the country

---

[34] For an insightful discussion of Takami's case, see Horikawa Keiko, "Koshukei wa Zangyaku ka", *Sekai*, No. 825 (January 2012), pp. 63–72, and *Sekai*, No. 827 (February 2012), pp. 122–131.

[35] Kenji Nagata and David T. Johnson, "Hanging in Japan: What Occupation Era Documents and a Lay Judge Trial Teach About the State That Still Kills in Secret", *Punishment & Society*, Vol. 16, No. 3 (July 2014), p. 247.

cannot escape some of the problems and paradoxes that have plagued execution methods in America. This conclusion focuses on four of them.[36]

First, there is no humane way to execute a human being. There is a large body of evidence documenting problems with capital punishment in America, from wrongful convictions and racial bias to geographic disparities and failures of deterrence. The evidence about capital punishment in Japan is more limited because the subject has been less researched, but it points to a similar conclusion, that the death penalty involves godlike actions without godlike wisdom or skills. It is impossible to construct a system of capital punishment that reaches only the rare, right cases, without also occasionally condemning the innocent or the undeserving. It is also impossible to construct a system of executions that takes the lives of heinous offenders in a manner that is humane. The United States has tried to do the latter—to realize the dream of a perfect execution—and it has failed.[37] Japan has hardly tried at all. One might call the Japanese approach a prudential form of "legal realism" or a wise refusal to be seduced by an "impossible dream." But one could also call it a failure of legal aspiration that parallels the tendency of the country's courts (described in Chapter 2) to assume that death is not a "different" form of punishment requiring special procedures and protections for the accused. In law as in life, failures of aspiration can be even more troubling than failures of performance.

Second, hanging in Japan raises a question about the difference between criminal violence and the violence that law employs to punish crime. In the United States, frequent efforts to improve execution methods are partly a search for a way of taking life that signals the superiority of state killing over the killings that citizens commit. After more than a half-century of silence about the propriety of hanging, Japan may now be starting its own search for a method of execution that tries to signal "superiority" of this kind. It remains to be seen how diligent Japan's

---

[36] Kenji Nagata and David T. Johnson, "Hanging in Japan: What Occupation Era Documents and a Lay Judge Trial Teach About the State That Still Kills in Secret", *Punishment & Society*, Vol. 16, No. 3 (July 2014), pp. 247–249.

[37] Timothy V. Kaufman-Osborn, "Perfect Execution: Abolitionism and the Paradox of Lethal Injection", in Charles J. Ogletree and Austin Sarat, editors, *The Road to Abolition: The Future of Capital Punishment in the United States* (New York University Press, 2009), pp. 215–251.

search will be, but the American experience provides ample reason for pessimism about the results.³⁸ At the same time, the Occupation documents and the Osaka trial suggest that as it relates to Japan, the question about the distinctiveness of law's violence may no longer be hanging in oblivion.

Third, efforts to reform how the state kills confront death penalty opponents in Japan with the same paradox that their American counterparts face. On the one hand, if attempts to challenge hanging are abandoned, there will be gratuitous suffering by people who are executed. On the other hand, if legal challenges to hanging in Japan continue, "victory" in the form of reform of execution methods will prove pyrrhic if it means complicity in the state's effort to accomplish the sort of anesthetized death that fosters collective amnesia about the violence of capital punishment. This, anyway, is what has happened in the United States.³⁹ Japanese death penalty reformers would be wise to recognize the risk of trying to change their country's execution method. Execution reform is often a two-edged sword, and "the better" (a "softer" method of execution) can be the enemy of "the best" (abolition).

Finally, the Japanese state continues to kill in secret, so little is known about how it hangs, but what we learn from the Occupation documents and the Osaka trial is troubling. Hanging in twenty-first-century Japan is no more humane than hanging in nineteenth-century Nagoya or Nagasaki. As for the future, there is little reason to expect Japan's Supreme Court to find hanging problematic for the simple reason that it rarely finds anything constitutionally suspect. Since its creation in 1947, Japan's top court has struck down fewer than 10 statutes on constitutional grounds.⁴⁰ By comparison, Germany's constitutional court, which was established several years later, has struck down over 600. The most promising venue for challenging the propriety of hanging in Japan is the court of public opinion. In the years to come, the country's lay

---

[38] Austin Sarat, *Gruesome Spectacles: Botched Executions and America's Death Penalty* (Stanford University Press, 2014).

[39] Deborah W. Denno, "For Execution Methods Challenges, the Road to Abolition Is Paved with Paradox", in Charles J. Ogletree and Austin Sarat, editors, *The Road to Abolition: The Future of Capital Punishment in the United States* (New York University, 2009), pp. 183–214.

[40] David S. Law, "The Anatomy of a Conservative Court: Judicial Review in Japan", *Texas Law Review*, Vol. 87, No. 7, pp. 1545–1594.

judge system will provide more opportunities for capital defendants and defense lawyers to raise questions about the legality and legitimacy of a method of execution that has hardly changed in a century and a half. Japanese governments have long acted as if state killing is state business, but now that citizens are participating in decisions about who to send to the gallows, they are wanting to know more about what happens *after* a sentence of death has been imposed. Surely some members of the Japanese media should be permitted to watch executions so that they can provide information for citizens to make more enlightened judgments about the reality of capital punishment. Until such reforms occur, secrecy will remain a problematic premise for administering the ultimate punishment.

Open Access This chapter is licensed under the terms of the Creative Commons Attribution-NonCommercial-NoDerivatives 4.0 International License (http://creativecommons.org/licenses/by-nc-nd/4.0/), which permits any noncommercial use, sharing, distribution and reproduction in any medium or format, as long as you give appropriate credit to the original author(s) and the source, provide a link to the Creative Commons license and indicate if you modified the licensed material. You do not have permission under this license to share adapted material derived from this chapter or parts of it.

The images or other third party material in this chapter are included in the chapter's Creative Commons license, unless indicated otherwise in a credit line to the material. If material is not included in the chapter's Creative Commons license and your intended use is not permitted by statutory regulation or exceeds the permitted use, you will need to obtain permission directly from the copyright holder.

CHAPTER 4

Wrongful Convictions and the Culture of Denial

Abstract On the surface, it appears the United States has a more serious problem with wrongful convictions than Japan, for it has uncovered many more cases of this kind. Yet this gap is probably more apparent than real, for Japan does a poor job of discovering wrongful convictions. To reduce the problem of wrongful convictions in Japanese criminal justice and capital punishment, reformers must make structural reforms, but they must also confront a "culture of denial" (*hitei no bunka*) that makes it difficult to acknowledge mistakes.

Keywords Hakamada Iwao · Wrongful conviction · Miscarriage of justice · Structural reform · Culture of denial

Hakamada Iwao was sentenced to death in 1968 for the murder of four people. He was released in 2014 because of evidence of his innocence. At the time of his arrest he was a young man. At the time of his release he was 78 years old—diabetic, deluded about his identity, and dimly aware of his own situation. In the five years since he was released, prosecutors have continued to claim that Hakamada is guilty, but as of this writing he remains free, living with his sister in the city of Hamamatsu, struggling to recover his health, and—as a matter of law—still a convicted killer under sentence of death. Time will tell whether Hakamada is formally acquitted at a retrial (which may or may not occur), but the three judges on the Shizuoka District Court who ordered his release left little doubt about their view:

> In addition to approving a retrial for the defendant, it is natural to suspend the execution of his death sentence. Moreover, based on this court's discretion, we conclude that it is also appropriate to suspend the execution of the defendant's confinement. This defendant has been convicted and incarcerated for an extremely long period of time under the threat of capital punishment based on important evidence that may well have been planted by the investigating authorities. At present, when the high probability of the defendant's innocence has been made clear, detaining him any longer would violate justice to an intolerable extent.[1]

I believe that Hakamada is innocent and that his confinement for almost half a century is an abomination of justice. I also believe that his case is not an isolated accident.[2] Wrongful convictions result from human and systemic errors that recur on a regular basis.[3] Hakamada's half-century nightmare resulted from the interaction of several such errors:

- Hakamada falsely confessed to crimes he did not commit. His admissions of guilt were coerced through interrogation practices that lasted more than 250 hours and that broke his will to resist.
- Japanese police apparently planted evidence—clothes in a miso tank near the scene of the crime—in order to frame Hakamada.
- Japanese prosecutors concealed from the defense more than 100 photographs and statements which might have cleared Hakamada decades before they finally acknowledged the existence of this critical evidence.
- Japanese media coverage of the four murders put pressure on police, prosecutors, and courts to produce a conviction. It also contributed to the "tunnel vision" and "confirmation bias" that afflicted legal officials in this case.

---

[1] David T. Johnson, "An Innocent Man: Hakamada Iwao and the Problem of Wrongful Convictions in Japan", *The Asia-Pacific Journal/Japan Focus*, Vol. 13 (2015), pp. 1–38.

[2] David T. Johnson, "Wrongful Convictions and the Culture of Denial in Japanese Criminal Justice", *The Asia-Pacific Journal/Japan Focus*, Vol. 13 (2015), pp. 1–10.

[3] Dan Simon, *In Doubt: The Psychology of the Criminal Justice Process* (Harvard University Press, 2012).

- Hakamada's trial failed to ascertain the accuracy of the evidence produced by police and prosecutors, and his defense lawyers contributed to this failure. Criminal trials provide a number of mechanisms that are supposed to safeguard the accuracy of verdicts, including the presumption of innocence, a burden of proof "beyond a reasonable doubt," vigorous cross-examination, and assurances that the adjudicators will be impartial and objective. All of these safeguards miscarried in Hakamada's case.
- For decades, Japan's appellate courts failed to acknowledge problems in Hakamada's case. In effect, they repeatedly ratified the foregoing errors while Hakamada lost his mind on death row.

A criminal case can go wrong in two main ways. A person who committed a crime may escape punishment, or a person may be convicted and punished for a crime that he or she did not commit. Every criminal justice system makes mistakes of both kinds, and most cultures and criminal justice professionals believe that the worst mistake is the false conviction of people who are actually innocent. As British jurist William Blackstone observed in the eighteenth century, "it is better that ten guilty persons escape than that one innocent suffer." An aversion to convicting the innocent is also well established in Japanese legal culture. Indeed, in Japan, even people who are arrested but *not convicted* are often deemed to be victims of a "miscarriage of justice" (*enzai*). This kind of criticism is seldom heard in the United States, where it is widely accepted that some people who get arrested will not be convicted. This difference suggests that in some respects Japanese people may be more sensitive than Americans to criminal injustice.

The problem of wrongful conviction in Japan cannot be understood without considering how it compares with other countries. Here as in many areas of social research, to know only one country is to know no country well. Comparison with the United States is especially instructive because there have been many studies of wrongful conviction there and because the United States and Japan are both developed democracies that retain capital punishment and continue to carry out executions on a regular basis. On the surface, the United States seems to have a more serious problem with wrongful convictions than Japan, for it has uncovered many more cases of this kind. But I believe this gap is more apparent than real, for Japan does a deplorable job of discovering wrongful convictions. To reduce the problem of wrongful convictions in Japanese criminal justice, reformers must confront a "culture of denial" (*hitei no bunka*) that makes it difficult for police, prosecutors, and judges to acknowledge their mistakes and that makes the public and the media complicit in their own dimsightedness.[4]

Wrongful Convictions in America and Europe

The United States has been the subject of more wrongful conviction research than any country in the world.[5] The results are troubling. From 1989 to 2017, more than 2100 persons were wrongfully convicted and subsequently released from prison because of evidence of their innocence.[6] That is 6 exonerations per month for 29 years (1 every 5 days). Forty-seven percent of these victims of wrongful conviction were African-American even though African-Americans make up only 13 percent of the U.S. population. Victims of wrongful conviction spent an average of 9 years in prison before being released, and many spent two or three times that long. About three-quarters were wrongfully convicted of homicide or sexual assault—crimes which tend to leave physical evidence behind that later can be tested, and crimes which attract more media attention than most criminal cases do. Less than one-quarter of these victims were exonerated based on DNA evidence, partly because biological evidence (saliva, semen, blood, and the like) is available in only 10–15 percent of serious felony cases. The leading causes of wrongful

---

[4] There are several good documentaries about wrongful convictions in Japan. One is about Hakamada, directed by Kim Sung-woong: "Yume no Ma no Yo no Naka" (Kimoon Film, 2016). See also Kim's "Sayama: Mienai Tejo o Hazusu made" (2013), about a *burakumin* man named Ishikawa Kazuo, who was released in 1994 after serving 31 years in prison, and who has been seeking a retrial ever since his conviction for the kidnapping and murder of a 16-year-old girl in 1963; and "Gokutomo" (2018), about friendships between five men, all of whom were convicted of murder: Hakamada Iwao (released from death row in 2014), Ishikawa Kazuo (released on parole in 1994), Sugaya Toshikazu (acquitted at retrial in 2009), Sakurai Shoji (acquitted at retrial in 2011), and Sugiyama Takao (acquitted at retrial in 2011).

[5] One exemplary work of scholarship on wrongful convictions in America is Mark Godsey, *Blind Justice: A Former Prosecutor Exposes the Psychology and Politics of Wrongful Convictions* (University of California Press, 2017). Another is Brandon L. Garrett, *Convicting the Innocent: Where Criminal Prosecutions Go Wrong* (Harvard University Press, 2011).

[6] The National Registry of Exonerations, at https://www.law.umich.edu/special/exoneration/Pages/about.aspx.

conviction in these cases were perjury and false accusation, official misconduct, mistaken witness testimony, false or misleading forensic evidence, and false confessions. All of these causes were operative in the wrongful conviction of Hakamada Iwao, and they have shipwrecked justice in other Japanese cases too.

All wrongful convictions are tragic, but the most worrisome are those that result in a mistaken sentence of death. From 1973 to 2018, 164 persons in 28 American states were released from death row because of evidence of their innocence.[7] That is an average of 3.6 death row exonerations per year for 46 years. More than half of these exonerations (84) were of black men, and more than half (83) occurred in just five states: Florida (28), Illinois (21), Texas (13), Louisiana (11), and Oklahoma (10). Many analysts believe that some wrongly condemned persons have been executed. For example, Carlos DeLuna, a poor Hispanic man with childlike intelligence, was executed in Texas in 1989 based on one, nighttime, cross-ethnic eyewitness identification with no corroborating forensic evidence.[8] There is a growing list of executed persons whose guilt has been called into serious doubt following post-execution investigations. America's wrongful executions may also include Ruben Cantu (executed in Texas in 1993), Larry Griffin (Missouri, 1995), David Spence (Texas, 1997), Claude Jones (Texas, 2000), and Cameron Todd Willingham (Texas, 2004). In 2015, the U.S. Justice Department and the FBI formally acknowledged that nearly every examiner in an FBI forensic squad overstated forensic hair matches for *two decades* before the year 2000. Of 28 forensic examiners who testified to hair matches in a total of 268 trials, 26 were found to have overstated the evidence, and 95 percent of the overstatements favored the prosecution. Defendants were sentenced to death in 12 percent of those trials.

While the foregoing figures are troubling, the true scale of America's wrongful conviction problem cannot be known because some wrongly convicted persons are never discovered. Educated estimates of the percentage of criminal cases resulting in wrongful conviction have been made, and they range from 3 to 5 percent in capital homicide cases, and

---

[7] Death Penalty Information Center, at https://deathpenaltyinfo.org/innocence-and-death-penalty.

[8] James S. Liebman and the Columbia DeLuna Project, *The Wrong Carlos: Anatomy of a Wrongful Conviction* (Columbia University Press, 2014).

8 percent or more in cases of sexual assault.[9] These estimates are much larger than criminal justice experts and professionals supposed before the "discovery of innocence" in the 1990s raised awareness of this problem in American criminal justice.[10] The steep decline of capital punishment in the United States since 2000—death sentences and executions have plummeted—has several causes, including a sharp decrease in the homicide rate and improved capital defense, but one of the most important causes seems to be concern about miscarriages of justice, which has made prosecutors, judges, juries, and governors more cautious about capital punishment.

The problem of innocence is hardly the only problem afflicting America's death penalty system. As Chapter 2 described, death sentences are also imposed on defendants who are guilty but do not deserve to be executed. A study of more than 4500 death sentences imposed between 1973 and 1995 found that 68 percent were overturned on appeal because of "serious reversible error" in the original trial. When these cases were retried, 82 percent resulted in a sentence less than death, and 7 percent ended in acquittal. Findings such as these suggest that the actual practice of American capital punishment has all the consistency of a lottery. Errors in finding facts and assessing culpability are so widespread that American capital punishment must be called "a broken system."[11]

The problem of wrongful convictions is serious in European countries too. In the former West Germany, for example, Dr. Karl Peters identified 1415 wrongful conviction cases between 1951 and 1964—an average of 101 wrongful convictions per year in a country that had 40 percent fewer people than Japan. The causes were much the same as those that have been identified by wrongful conviction researchers in the United States.[12]

---

[9] Dan Simon, *In Doubt: The Psychology of the Criminal Justice Process* (Harvard University Press, 2012), p. 4.

[10] Frank R. Baumgartner, Suzanna L. De Boef, and Amber E. Boydstun, *The Decline of the Death Penalty and the Discovery of Innocence* (Cambridge University Press, 2008).

[11] James S. Liebman, Jeffrey Fagan, and Valerie West, "A Broken System: Error Rates in Capital Cases, 1973–1995", https://papers.ssrn.com/sol3/papers.cfm?abstract_id=232712.

[12] See Nose Hiroyuki, et al., *Gohan no Kenkyu: Nishi Doitsu no Saishin Jirei no Bunseki* (Hokkaido Daigaku Toshokankokai, 1981). Dr. Peters' study was originally published in Germany in 1974.

The wheels of all criminal justice systems are turned by the same imperfect operations of human beings: memory, recognition, inference, social influence, self-interest, and so on. Criminal verdicts in Germany, the United States, Japan, and other countries can be no better than the combined result of these flawed human activities.[13]

Yet the risk of convicting innocent people is not equal across nations. There is variation from country to country within the European Union, and the risk of wrongful conviction in the United States is probably greater than in most countries of Western Europe because American systems of adversarial criminal justice strike a different balance between the need to obtain convictions and the need to find the truth than do inquisitorial criminal justice systems on the European continent. American criminal justice also relies on plea bargaining to dispose of more than 90 percent of all criminal cases, and errors in fact-finding may be more frequent in cases handled this way than in those that go to trial. For these reasons, wrongful convictions appear to be more frequent in the United States than in countries such as Germany, France, and Holland, even when taking into account differences in population and caseload.[14]

Wrongful Convictions in Japan

Nobody knows how many persons have been wrongfully convicted in Japan, and even educated estimates are rare because few decent studies have been done. One recent effort to count identified 162 cases of confirmed or strongly suspected wrongful conviction between 1910 and 2010, all of which were discovered in the postwar period, and more than half of which involved homicide.[15] See Table 4.1. In this century-long

---

[13] Dan Simon, *In Doubt: The Psychology of the Criminal Justice Process* (Harvard University Press, 2012).

[14] On wrongful convictions in comparative perspective, see the studies in these two books: C. Ronald Huff and Martin Killias, editors, *Wrongful Conviction: International Perspectives on Miscarriages of Justice* (Temple University Press, 2008); and C. Ronald Huff and Martin Killias, editors, *Wrongful Convictions and Miscarriages of Justice: Causes and Remedies in North American and European Criminal Justice Systems* (Routledge, 2013).

[15] Makoto Ibusuki and Nichibenren Enzai Gen'in Kyumei Daisansha Kikan Wakingu Gurupu, editors, *Enzai Gen'in o Chosa Seyo: Kokkai ni Daisansha Kikan no Setchi o* (Keiso Shobo, 2012), pp. 155–168.

Table 4.1 Wrongful convictions in Japan by decade, 1910–2010

Decade	Number
1910s	2
1920s	1
1930s	0
1940s	13
1950s	37
1960s	14
1970s	31
1980s	31
1990s	16
2000s	17
Total, 1910–2010	162

Source Makoto Ibusuki and Nichibenren Enzai Gen'in Kyumei Daisansha Kikan Wakingu Gurupu, editors, *Enzai Gen'in o Chosa Seyo: Kokkai ni Daisansha Kikan no Setchi o* (Keiso Shobo, 2012), pp. 155–168

survey, the average number of wrongful convictions per decade is 16, with a high of 37 in the 1950s and lows of 2 or fewer in the 1910s, the 1920s, and the 1930s. But of course, 162 wrongful convictions in one century is surely a major undercount. In my view, this number probably represents the "tip of an iceberg" of wrongful convictions in Japan, for three reasons: because old wrongful conviction cases are difficult to document (the prewar totals are implausibly low); because less serious crimes (such as drug offenses) fell outside the scope of this study; and most fundamentally, because many cases of wrongful conviction are never discovered at all. We therefore need to ask: how big is the rest of Japan's iceberg?

Since 1945, only ten persons have been sentenced to death or life imprisonment in Japan and subsequently acquitted at retrial. Hakamada Iwao could become number eleven, if he receives a retrial (prosecutors are resisting) and if he does not die before a retrial is completed. This is an average of one exoneration every seven years—a small fraction of the frequency in the United States. The tiny number allows two contrasting interpretations.[16]

---

[16] David T. Johnson, "Wrongful Convictions and the Culture of Denial in Japanese Criminal Justice", *The Asia-Pacific Journal/Japan Focus*, Vol. 13 (2015), pp. 3–4.

On the one hand, Japanese prosecutors tend to be cautious about charging cases. In fact, a conservative charging policy—to avoid taking defendants to trial who could be acquitted—is one of the main reasons for the country's high conviction rate. This charging policy is enforced through organizational mechanisms such as a *kessai* system of hierarchical consultation and review, whereby front-line prosecutors consult with their superiors about the propriety of their charge and sentence-request decisions, and a tendency to punish prosecutors who charge or try cases that end in acquittal—especially if their decision-making was deemed defective.[17] On this view, Japan *produces* relatively few wrongful convictions because prosecutors send fewer innocent persons to trial than do their counterparts in the United States and other countries with higher acquittal rates.

The second explanation for the low number of wrongful convictions revealed in Japan stresses their *discovery*, not their production. On this view, Japan has relatively few actors or institutions that focus on finding wrongful convictions, and hence few are found. Japan has relatively few lawyers, only a handful of whom concentrate on criminal defense. The major national newspapers do little investigative reporting (contrast *Yomiuri* and *Asahi* with *The New York Times* or *The Guardian*). Few Japanese scholars seriously study the subject of wrongful conviction. Japan's appellate courts tend to defer to law enforcement interests and ratify the status quo.[18] Japan has no exoneration registries and only established its first Innocence Project in 2016 (at Ritsumeikan University in Kyoto). And Japan has no case review commissions, except for the Japan Federation of Bar Association's Committee for the Protection of Human Rights, which has done good work in some cases, and which has published two reports (in 1998 and 2009), but which is not capable of providing assistance to all of the victims of wrongful conviction in the world's eleventh most populous country.

In sum, the number of wrongful convictions revealed in a country depends on how many have been produced *and* on how effectively

---

[17] David T. Johnson, *The Japanese Way of Justice: Prosecuting Crime in Japan* (Oxford University Press, 2002), pp. 237–242.

[18] Daniel H. Foote, "Policymaking by the Japanese Judiciary in the Criminal Justice Field", *Hoshakaigaku*, No. 72, pp. 6–45.

they have been found. Japan's institutional shortcomings suggest that its wrongful conviction problem is larger than it appears. When Kitani Akira was a judge in Japan, he sometimes acquitted two or three defendants a year—and he acquitted about 30 defendants throughout the course of his career. Not a single acquittal was overturned on appeal.[19] Is it plausible that hundreds of other Japanese judges can go year after year without issuing an acquittal—and without wrongfully convicting a single defendant? Surveys of Japanese lawyers in 1989 and 1999 suggest the answer is no, for in each of those years more than 40 percent of respondents said they had handled cases in which a wrongful conviction occurred.[20] Similarly, Takano Takashi (a prominent defense lawyer) believes Japan's true total of wrongful convictions is much larger than the small number that has been officially recognized. On his analysis, Japan may produce as many as 1500 wrongful convictions (*enzai*) each year, almost none of which is officially recognized.[21] In the years since Takano made this estimate, Japan's acquittal rate has not significantly changed, though prosecutors have become more cautious about charging cases in the lay judge system that took effect in 2009, as will be described in the next chapter.

Structural Reforms

Compared to the United States, Japan has not discovered many wrongful convictions, but in recent years a small stream of wrongful convictions has surfaced, including Sugaya Toshikazu, Yanagihara Hiroshi, Govinda Mainali, Sakurai Shoji, Sugiyama Takao, Boku Tatsuhiro, and Aoki Keiko. To some observers, these cases suggest that Japan is where the United States was 25 years ago—just waking up to the problem of "actual innocence" in its criminal justice system.[22] Whether Japan experiences its own

---

[19] Kitani Akira, *"Muzai" o Minuku: Saibankan Kitani Akira no Ikikata* (Iwanami Shoten, 2013), p. 247.

[20] Japan Federation of Bar Associations, "Atarashii Seiki no Keiji Tetsuzuki o Motomete" (JFBA, 1999), p. 506.

[21] Takano Takashi, "Jijitsu Nintei wa Shimin ni Makaseta Hoga Yoi", Keiji Saiban o Kangaeru blog, January 7, 2007, and "Nihon no Kensatsu wa Hetare na no ka", Keiji Saiban o Kangaeru blog, June 14 and June 23, 2009.

[22] See the Japan Innocence and Death Penalty Information Center http://www.jiadep.org/About_JIADEP.html, which is managed by Hyogo University Professor Michael H. Fox.

"innocence revolution" will depend on what reforms occur in the years to come.²³ In thinking about the future, it is important to remember the past. In the 1980s, four men—Menda Sakae, Taniguchi Shigeyoshi, Saito Sachio, and Akabori Masao—were released from death row because of evidence of their innocence. Afterward, many proposals were made for reform of Japan's criminal justice system, but in all fundamental respects the system remained unchanged.²⁴ A 229-page report by the Supreme Prosecutors Office did not even acknowledge that prosecutors were wrong to indict these defendants. In the aftermath of more recent miscarriages of justice, Japan's penchant for conservative reform has been on display once again.²⁵ In 2010, for example, who expected that the revelation of serious prosecutorial misconduct in the case of Muraki Atsuko, a senior official in the health ministry who was framed by prosecutors in Osaka and subsequently acquitted, would lead to *expanded* powers for prosecutors to plea bargain, wiretap, and grant immunity? Yet that is what happened in 2016, when Japan's Code of Criminal Procedure was revised to further enable these practices. In Japanese criminal justice, the more things change, the more they stay the same.²⁶

Wrongful convictions are often caused by conformity to standard operating procedures. In many respects, the problem is systems, not devils.²⁷ Hence, addressing the problem of wrongful convictions requires systemic and structural reforms. For starters, Japan needs to develop better institutions for finding wrongful convictions after they occur. In this respect, Japan remains well behind the United States and England. The study of wrongful convictions also needs to become more important in Japan's legal academy. For this to happen, funders must make the subject a higher research priority.

---

²³ Harada Kunio, *Gyakuten Muzai no Jijitsu Nintei* (Keizo Shobo, 2012).

²⁴ Daniel H. Foote, "From Japan's Death Row to Freedom", *Pacific Rim Law & Policy Journal*, Vol. 1, No. 1 (1992), p. 102; and Daniel H. Foote, "The Door That Never Opens: Capital Punishment and Post-conviction Review of Death Sentences in the United States and Japan", *Brooklyn Journal of International Law*, Vol. 19, No. 2 (1993), pp. 367–521.

²⁵ Suo Masayuki, *Sore demo Boku wa Kaigi de Tatakau: Dokyumento Keiji Shiho Kaikaku* (Iwanami, 2015).

²⁶ As Giuseppe Tomasi di Lampudesa has the Prince's nephew say in *The Leopard*, "If we want things to stay as they are, things will have to change" (London: Fontana, 1963), p. 27.

²⁷ James M. Doyle, "The Real Culprits in the Central Park 5 Convictions", *The Crime Report*, July 8, 2019.

Wrongful convictions must also be prevented before they occur. To do so, Japan should implement internationally recognized "best practices" in its criminal justice system, the most important of which is a requirement to electronically record all criminal interrogations in their entirety. Japan has made progress in this direction, but much more needs to be done. The 2016 revision to the Code of Criminal Procedure made it mandatory for police and prosecutors to video record interrogation in cases that will be handled by lay judge trials and in cases that are independently initiated by prosecutors, but these account for only 2 to 3 percent of all criminal cases in the country. The new law also allows investigators to forego recording if they believe recording will inhibit suspects from making meaningful statements, and it imposes no obligation to record statements made by people being questioned on a voluntary basis either prior to arrest or after indictment. These loopholes are so large that they could swallow the principle of transparency to which they are supposed to be exceptions.

When a wrongful conviction occurs in Japan, a false confession is usually the primary proximate cause. One study found that "a confession was part of the evidence marshaled against defendants in 84 percent (42 out of 50) of the confirmed *enzai* cases between 1945 and 1991 in which a conviction was later overturned."[28] This is a much higher percentage than in American exonerations. False confessions were also centrally relevant in all four of the Japanese death penalty cases that ended in retrial and acquittal in the 1980s, and in Hakamada's half-century nightmare as well. Yet in the Special Committee on Criminal Justice for a New Era (*Shinjidai no Keiji Shiho Seido Tokubetsubukai*), which ostensibly aimed to address some of the problems exposed by the aforementioned prosecutorial scandal, "sweet-talking for the government" by prominent Japanese professors resulted in remarkably lax recommendations for reform—reform that could have created substantially more transparency and accountability in Japan's interrogation rooms. But instead,

---

[28] John H. Davis, "Courting Justice, Contesting 'Bureaucratic Informality': The Sayama Case and the Evolution of Buraku Liberation Politics", in Patricia G. Steinhoff, editor, *Going to Court to Change Japan: Social Movements and the Law in Contemporary Japan* (Center for Japanese Studies at the University of Michigan, 2014), p. 76.

interrogation rooms remain some of the most closed and secretive spaces in Japanese society.[29]

There are many good reasons to record interrogations, and no good reasons not to. Compared to other democracies, this need is especially great in Japan, where interrogations are long and the suspect's right to silence is undermined by a "duty to endure questioning."[30] Because electronic recording is a medium for preserving the truth of interrogations and confessions, it serves what is widely regarded as the cardinal objective of Japanese criminal justice: truth-finding. Recording also serves the interests of all the parties in the criminal process. Defendants and defense attorneys benefit because recording deters impermissible interrogation techniques and helps prevent wrongful convictions based on false confessions. Police and prosecutors benefit because recording protects them against false accusations of impropriety and abuse. And judges and lay judges benefit because recording gives them the information they need to assess the voluntariness and veracity of confessions.

Prosecutors must also become more transparent about the evidence in their possession, and Japanese history suggests they will not do so voluntarily. Since the "Conspiracy at Matsukawa" case[31] that resulted in the wrongful conviction of 20 men in 1950 and their subsequent acquittal, it appears that every exoneration in Japan has been preceded by the failure of prosecutors to disclose critical evidence to the defense. In Hakamada's case, that failure endured for decades. In this respect, Japan's procuracy may be less transparent today than it was before the Occupation, when prosecutors were required to disclose all dossiers to the defense, not just the statements they submitted as evidence at trial.[32]

The evidence in a criminal case is not owned by the state. It is a public good, and state officials should be required to share it with the

---

[29] Suo Masayuki, *Sore demo Boku wa Kaigi de Tatakau: Dokyumento Keiji Shiho Kaikaku* (Iwanami, 2015).

[30] On criminal interrogation in Japan, see Setsuo Miyazawa, *Policing in Japan: A Study on Making Crime* (State University of New York Press, 1992); and Daniel H. Foote, "Confessions and the Right to Silence in Japan", *Georgia Journal of International and Comparative Law*, Vol. 21 (1991), pp. 415–488. On criminal interrogation in the United States, see Richard A. Leo, *Police Interrogation and American Justice* (Harvard University Press, 2008).

[31] Chalmers Johnson, *Conspiracy at Matsukawa* (University of California Press, 1972).

[32] David T. Johnson, *The Japanese Way of Justice: Prosecuting Crime in Japan* (Oxford University Press, 2002), p. 272.

defense.³³ But prosecutors in Japan have worked hard to delimit the defense's rights to discovery, and its justifications have been self-serving. For an organization that trumpets the importance of truth-telling so much, it is ironic that the procuracy opposes disclosing to the defense more of the building blocks—draft dossiers especially—that front-line prosecutors use to construct "the truth" they advocate at trial.³⁴ The present system also relies inordinately on the goodwill of prosecutors to disclose relevant evidence to the defense, though occasionally they are spurred to do so by "recommendations" from the bench. In Shizuoka, repeated nudges by judges led to the belated disclosure of evidence to Hakamada's defense lawyers and ultimately to release of the world's longest incarcerated inmate on death row. To prevent more miscarriages of that kind, prosecutors should be required to disclose all of the evidence in their possession to the defense before a trial starts. In some parts of the United States and in other jurisdictions, this is called "full file disclosure."

As described in Chapter 2, Japanese legal professionals—prosecutors, judges, and defense lawyers—frequently emphasize the need to be "cautious" (*shincho*) about capital punishment. But if Ministers of Justice and prosecutors were serious about this assertion, they would seek reforms that recognize how justice can miscarry. Recording interrogations in their entirety and disclosing all evidence to the defense would reduce the risk of wrongful conviction in Japanese criminal justice. Until these reforms are realized, claims about the need to be "cautious" will sound like empty rhetoric.

A Culture of Denial

The structural reforms described above are essential, but without a change in Japan's culture of criminal justice they will have limited impact. Reforming institutions is the main means of change in the modern approach to developing democracy, but the notion that structural

---

³³ Makoto Ibusuki, "Subete no Shoko Kaiji o Isoge: Hakamada Jiken no Kyokun", *Asahi Shimbun*, May 9, 2014.

³⁴ David T. Johnson, *The Japanese Way of Justice: Prosecuting Crime in Japan* (Oxford University Press, 2002), pp. 98–99.

reform alters actual practice is more hope than fact.[35] Research on "making democracy work" warns that the "designers of new institutions are often writing on water."[36] That is, culture and history strongly condition the effectiveness of new rules and institutions, and long-established norms can limit the possibilities for achieving structural reform. Because culture counts, addressing the problem of wrongful convictions must attend to this area too. The most important imperative concerns cultural assumptions that are relevant in many areas of Japanese society, from aviation and medicine to nuclear energy and criminal justice. Three principles are primary.[37]

First, in order to reduce error one must assume it is inevitable. When I started studying criminal justice in Japan in the early 1990s, prosecutors told me that the miscarriages of justice that happened in the first decade or so after the Pacific War "could not occur anymore" because they were caused by an immature system of criminal justice that had been radically reformed during the Occupation and that was still working out its problems in the early postwar period. Subsequent events revealed that claim to be false. Japan continues to have problems with wrongful conviction, and the most serious problem involves a culture of denial that makes it difficult for police, prosecutors, and judges to acknowledge their own mistakes and for the media and other external agents of accountability to conduct rigorous investigations.[38] Because this culture of denial shields those actors from pain, humiliation, and change, it is easy to understand why they cling to it. Letting the culture of denial go and embracing the lessons that error can teach will require honor and courage. It also will require pressure from Japanese society—and from political leaders especially. Culture, not politics, often determines the success of legal reforms, though politics can change a culture and save it from itself.[39]

---

[35] Bent Flyvbjerg, *Rationality and Power: Democracy in Practice* (University of Chicago Press, 1998).

[36] Robert Putnam, *Making Democracy Work: Civic Traditions in Modern Italy* (Princeton University Press, 1993), p. 17.

[37] For more details, see Kathryn Schulz's brilliant book *Being Wrong: Adventures in the Margin of Error* (Ecco, 2010), pp. 304–307.

[38] Hiromasa Ezoe, *Where Is the Justice? Media Attacks, Prosecutorial Abuse, and My 13 Years in Japanese Court* (Kodansha, 2010).

[39] Lawrence E. Harrison, *The Central Liberal Truth: How Politics Can Change a Culture and Save It From Itself* (Oxford University Press, 2006).

Second, in fields like medicine and aviation, successful strategies for error prevention rely on principles of openness and transparency to identify and learn from mistakes.[40] In contrast, Japan's system of criminal justice is so hostile to outside scrutiny that it remains impossible to see or say what many of its problems are. Most interrogations are not electronically recorded. It is all but impossible to do field research on policing. Prosecutors possess broad discretion to withhold evidence from the defense, and they are not reluctant to hide evidence when it serves their own interests. Lay judges are not permitted to discuss case details or deliberations even after their service has ended. And Japan's system for administering executions is surrounded by secrecy that is taken to extremes not seen in other nations. The insularity of Japanese criminal justice reflects the mistaken assumption that criminal proceedings are the special province of legal professionals. Whether Japan experiences its own "innocence revolution" depends partly on how transparent its criminal justice system becomes. At present, there may be no democratic country in the world where criminal justice is more closed.

The third cultural principle of error prevention is reliance on data so that criminal justice can be administered based on facts rather than on opinions, assumptions, and the prerogatives of power. But since empirical criminology is not well developed in Japan, little is known about how Japanese criminal justice is patterned. One key cause of this ignorance is the resistance of Japanese criminal justice officials to being studied in a serious way. Some Japanese scholars have experienced this resistance firsthand—and so have I. Several years ago I went to Tokyo to do research about policing in Kabukicho in the Shinjuku district. I was relying on the promise of an executive in the National Police Agency, that I would be given meaningful access to study police patrol activity in Japan's largest red light district. Despite several months of my best efforts, the promised access never materialized. I was given plenty of official police publications, and lots of bows and handshakes, but when I was permitted to do any field research at all, it consisted of standing outside police boxes (*koban*) in safe suburban settings such as Fuchu, far removed from the action I was interested in. And all the while I was in the "field,"

---

[40] James M. Doyle, "Learning from Error in the Criminal Justice System: Sentinel Event Reviews", in National Institute of Justice, *Mending Justice: Sentinel Event Reviews* (U.S. Department of Justice, September 2014), pp. 3–18.

I was watched by police-handlers from the Tokyo Metropolitan Police Department, who seemed as bored with their assignment to manage this foreigner as I was with my own meager access to their world.

Police are the most understudied actors in Japanese criminal justice.[41] This is ironic and unfortunate, for they are also the most important actors in Japan's criminal process. That criminal process is only as good as the evidence on which it feeds, and it is Japanese police who collect most of the evidence which informs criminal justice decision-making. Yet in Japan, hardly anyone studies police in a serious way. As one Japanese journalist observed:

> If a prominent sociologist from the West...came here to research the Japanese police, that scholar undoubtedly would conclude that this country is 'a strange land.' First he would run into the police wall of secrecy, and he would be unable to investigate actual police practices and conditions. Next he would be informed that there is no investigative reporting about the police by newspaper or other mainstream journalists, and that there are very few free-lance journalists who follow police issues. Then he would learn that in Japanese colleges and universities there are no courses about the police (as there are in the West) and no scholars who seriously study them. In the end, our friend the sociologist would discover that citizens and taxpayers (who have entrusted their safety to the police) have an extremely weak consciousness to try to check the police. Such a scholar, I think, would be seized by this question: Is Japan really a democratic country?[42]

Two decades after this passage was published, Japan remains a "strange land" with respect to research on police. Without decent data about them, reporters, citizens, and elected officials will remain easily manipulated by the public relations efforts of Japan's most powerful government agency.

Toxic to Justice

Wrongful convictions are inevitable in all criminal justice systems, but they can be significantly curtailed. In the United States, police or prosecutors initiate or cooperate in more than half of all exonerations, and

---

[41] David T. Johnson, "Policing in Japan", in James D. Babb, editor, *The Sage Handbook of Modern Japanese Studies* (Sage, 2015), pp. 222–243.

[42] M. Kobayashi, *Nihon Keisatsu no Genzai* (Iwanami Shoten, 1998), p. vi.

about 30 prosecutors' offices across the country have created "conviction integrity units" (CIUs) to review wrongful conviction claims.[43] Of the 166 exonerations that occurred in America in 2016, 70 came from CIUs. One of the first CIUs was created in Dallas in 2007 under Craig Watkins, an African-American District Attorney who grew concerned about the alarming number of miscarriages of justice that had been revealed in his jurisdiction. Since then, more than 90 percent of CIU exonerations have occurred in four large counties: Harris (Houston, Texas), Dallas (Texas), Cook (Chicago, Illinois), and Kings (Brooklyn, New York). The concentration of exonerations in a few CIUs suggests that some CIUs are more effective than others at uncovering wrongful convictions. One of the best models is in Brooklyn, where 10 full-time prosecutors work on more than 100 cases at any given time. As of the end of 2017, 23 people had been exonerated in Brooklyn, and of the cases reviewed there, 50 involved the bad behavior of a single retired detective named Louis Scarcella, who put away innocent people on false charges, over decades, by whatever means necessary—forced confessions, witness tampering, and a callous disregard for fairness and justice.[44]

The more open orientation to mistakes now seen in American CIUs is a marked break from the culture of denial that long characterized prosecution in the United States, and it also helps explain why there have been so many more exonerations in America than in Japan. America still has a long way to go to adequately address its problem with wrongful convictions, but the increased willingness to acknowledge error and learn from mistakes must be reckoned one of the most welcome developments in the past half-century of American criminal justice. By contrast, exonerations in Japan are almost always achieved despite strong resistance from police and prosecutors, and Japanese judges are frequently slow to acknowledge error as well (while Hakamada Iwao was detained on death row, more than a dozen judges rejected his appeals). If prosecutors in Japan are really the champions of justice that they claim to be, shouldn't they be creating CIU-like institutions that proactively search for errors?

---

[43] See "Conviction Integrity Units", at the National Registry of Exonerations webpage, https://www.law.umich.edu/special/exoneration/Pages/Conviction-Integrity-Units.aspx.

[44] For more on recent changes in American prosecution, see Emily Bazelon, *Charged: The New Movement to Transform American Prosecution and End Mass Incarceration* (Random House, 2019).

It is often said that "to err is human," but once a mistake has been made, humans have a choice between "covering up" and "fessing up." In June 2018, the Tokyo High Court overturned the ruling that had released Hakamada from death row because of evidence of his innocence, though the octogenarian was allowed to retain his freedom until the case returns to the Supreme Court. The next month, Japanese prosecutors exhorted the Supreme Court to reject Hakamada's appeal and to "stop this situation in which his sentence of death is suspended unnecessarily." Prosecutors' position appears to have two main causes: a desire to protect their individual and collective reputations, and a tendency toward tunnel vision, which leads them to dismiss evidence that is inconsistent with their preferred outcome ("guilty!") as irrelevant, incredible, or unreliable.

A path-breaking study of what it means to "be wrong" points out that if you recognize that errors are inevitable, you will not be surprised when they occur and you will have plans in place to correct them.[45] Conversely, if you refuse to admit that mistakes do occur, then every mistake—and every revelation of a wrongful conviction—becomes stark and humiliating evidence of how wrong you are. In this sense, Japan's culture of denial is toxic to justice, and so is the self-righteous certainty of criminal justice officials concerning the propriety of their own conduct. Doubt is a skill they still need to learn, and error is a reality they must learn to acknowledge. But they will not learn these lessons on their own. How long will Japanese society tolerate the status quo? And when will this country take an interest in the iceberg?

---

[45] Kathryn Schulz, *Being Wrong: Adventures in the Margin of Error* (Ecco, 2010), especially Chapter 14 on "The Paradox of Error".

Open Access This chapter is licensed under the terms of the Creative Commons Attribution-NonCommercial-NoDerivatives 4.0 International License (http://creativecommons.org/licenses/by-nc-nd/4.0/), which permits any noncommercial use, sharing, distribution and reproduction in any medium or format, as long as you give appropriate credit to the original author(s) and the source, provide a link to the Creative Commons license and indicate if you modified the licensed material. You do not have permission under this license to share adapted material derived from this chapter or parts of it.

The images or other third party material in this chapter are included in the chapter's Creative Commons license, unless indicated otherwise in a credit line to the material. If material is not included in the chapter's Creative Commons license and your intended use is not permitted by statutory regulation or exceeds the permitted use, you will need to obtain permission directly from the copyright holder.

CHAPTER 5

Capital Punishment and Lay Participation

Abstract This chapter examines two new forms of lay participation in Japanese capital justice. The lay judge reform of 2009 has stimulated many changes in formal rules and standard operating procedures in Japan's criminal process. These changes may be shifting the balance of power in Japanese criminal justice—a balance that has long favored law enforcement interests. Yet before and after the lay judge reform there are striking continuities in criminal justice outcomes, in conviction rates, punishment patterns, and death sentencing. The second reform is a victim participation system, which moves victims and survivors closer to center stage of Japan's criminal process, and which reflects and reinforces a culture of vengeance. Together, these two forms of lay participation may be doing as much to entrench capital punishment in Japan as to challenge and change it.

Keywords Lay judge system · Victim participation system · Burden · Closure · Culture of vengeance

One of the most striking facts about the death penalty in Japan is the dearth of significant change. The contrasts with America are stark. In the United States, public support for the death penalty has fallen to its lowest levels since the 1960s. Death sentences and executions have declined by about 80 percent since the 1990s. Nine states have abolished the death penalty since 2007 (making a total of 21), and in 4 other states governors have declared a moratorium on executions. Executions in several other states have been stopped because of botched executions and problems obtaining the chemicals used in lethal injection. The U.S. Supreme Court has prohibited execution of the mentally disabled and of juveniles. And of the more than 8000 death sentences imposed in the United States between 1973 and 2013, only 16 percent—about 1 in 6—resulted in execution. Most of the rest were overturned on appeal, commuted, or exonerated. So much change has occurred that some analysts believe the death penalty in America is "at the end of its rope" and that it will be abolished "not in a matter of generations, but in a matter of years."[1]

In Japan one sees far more continuity in death penalty policy and practice. Public support for capital punishment remains around 80 percent. Death sentences and executions continue to occur on a regular basis. There has been no extended moratorium on executions since a 40-month one ended in 1993—more than a quarter-century ago.[2] Japan's Supreme Court has done little to develop a meaningful jurisprudence of capital punishment. Most people sentenced to death get executed. And few serious observers believe abolition is near.

The previous three chapters explained why there has been so little death penalty change in Japan. When death is not deemed a different form of punishment, appellate courts seldom find reason to reverse death sentences, and the public remains convinced that capital punishment is a righteous response to heinous crime (Chapter 2). When the state kills in secret, nobody knows when executions are botched, and the public remains confident that the state kills decently (Chapter 3). And when a culture of denial results in the revelation of few wrongful convictions, most people remain untroubled by the possibility of error in life-and-death decision-making, and most leaders do little to address problems in the system (Chapter 4). This chapter explores the possibilities for change in Japanese capital punishment that could come from two reforms that took effect in 2009: a lay judge system that gives citizens a direct voice

---

[1] Brandon L. Garrett, *End of Its Rope: How Killing the Death Penalty Can Revive Criminal Justice* (Harvard University Press, 2017), p. 1.

[2] Mika Obara-Minnitt, *Japanese Moratorium on the Death Penalty* (Palgrave Macmillan, 2016).

in death penalty decision-making, and a victim participation system that moves crime victims and survivors closer to center stage of the criminal process. Since both reforms are relatively recent, it will take more time to discern their full effects. So far, however, they seem to be doing more to entrench capital punishment in Japan than to change or challenge it.[3]

A Stone into the Pond?

In 2009, Japan began a new trial system in which six lay persons sit with three professional judges to adjudicate guilt and determine sentence for murder and some other serious offenses.[4] The lay judge system puts citizen participation at the center of Japanese criminal trials (and death penalty decision-making) for the first time since 1943, when Japan's original Jury Act was suspended after fifteen years of fitful use (fewer than 500 jury trials were held in the 15 years before suspension).[5] Some analysts believe this trial reform will remake the country's criminal justice system. As they see it, the lay judge system has thrown "a stone into the pond" of criminal justice, and the ripples are gradually spreading.[6]

Several changes in the criminal process have been stimulated by the lay judge reform.[7] Since citizens cannot be asked to serve in court for long periods of time, a pretrial process was created to narrow and define the issues to be contested at trial. This has led to some improvement in the amount of evidence that prosecutors disclose to the defense before a trial begins, though more disclosure is needed. There also has been

---

[3] David T. Johnson, "Capital Punishment Without Capital Trials in Japan's Lay Judge System", *The Asia-Pacific Journal/Japan Focus*, Vol. 7 (2009), pp. 1–40.

[4] David T. Johnson, "Japan's Lay Judge System", in Jacqueline E. Ross and Stephen C. Thaman, editors, *Comparative Criminal Procedure* (Elgar, 2016), pp. 396–421.

[5] Dimitri Vanoverbeke, *Juries in the Japanese Legal System: The Coming Struggle for Citizen Participation and Democracy* (Routledge, 2015).

[6] See, for example, Shinomiya Satoru, "Defying Experts' Predictions, Identifying Themselves as Sovereign: Citizens' Responses to Their Service as Lay Judges in Japan", *Social Science Japan*, No. 43 (September 2010), pp. 8–13.

[7] For impact studies of the lay judge reform in Japan, see Erik Herber, *Lay and Expert Contributions to Japanese Criminal Justice* (Routledge, 2019, especially Chapter 6 on "Lay Judges and Sentencing"); and Rieko Kage, *Who Judges? Designing Jury Systems in Japan, East Asia, and Europe* (Cambridge University Press, 2017, especially Chapter 9 on "The Impact of New Lay Judge Systems").

progress toward recording interrogations, though more should be done here too. Bail has become easier to obtain as judges recognize the dangers of "kidnap justice" (*hitojichi shiho*), whereby pretrial detention is ruled necessary for most defendants who do not confess. Trials are easier to understand and more interesting than they used to be, for they are less reliant on the written statements (*chosho*) that are composed by police and prosecutors behind the closed doors of an interrogation room. Access to defense lawyers has improved, especially in the critical pretrial period when investigators focus on making suspects confess. One result is that suspects have become less cooperative, as more than 80 percent of prosecutors affirmed in a 2011 survey. Bar associations are training defense lawyers to become more effective advocates at trial. And so on.[8] These changes in procedure could transform death penalty decision-making by making citizens more aware of the reality of capital punishment. As U.S. Supreme Court Justice Thurgood Marshall posited in 1972, many people support capital punishment partly because they are ignorant about it. On this so-called "Marshall hypothesis", when people learn more about capital punishment, they come to regard it as immoral and unnecessary. But this kind of learning takes time. If the lay judge reform is going to transform capital punishment, it will be by evolution, not revolution.[9]

Deep change in Japanese capital punishment is hardly guaranteed. For one thing, civilian participation could be marginalized by legal professionals—prosecutors and judges especially—who aim to maintain their standard operating procedures. Indeed, marginalization into obscurity has happened several times in the past when reforms tried to make citizen participation a more central part of Japan's criminal process. The most striking examples are the prewar jury system and the postwar Prosecution Review Commissions, both of which had little effect on the actual practice of criminal justice.[10]

---

[8] Shinomiya Satoru, "Kokumin no Shutai teki – Jisshitsu teki Sanka wa Jitsugen Shite Iru ka: Saibanin Seido Shikko 10nen to Kongo no Kadai", *Jiyu to Seigi*, Vol. 70, No. 5 (May 2019), pp. 8–17.

[9] David T. Johnson and Setsuo Miyazawa, "Japanese Court Reform on Trial", in Rosann Greenspan, Hadar Aviram, and Jonathan Simon, editors, *The Legal Process and the Promise of Justice: Studies Inspired by the Work of Malcolm Feeley* (Cambridge University Press, 2019), pp. 122–138.

[10] Kent Anderson and Mark Nolan, "Lay Participation in the Japanese Justice System: A Few Preliminary Thoughts Regarding the Lay Assessor System (*saiban-in seido*) from

There are three signs that lay judges may be getting marginalized in the new trial system too. First, Japan's high conviction rate has not significantly declined. In comparable cases, the conviction rate went from 99.4 percent in 2006–2008 to 99.1 percent in 2009–2018.[11] Second, sentencing patterns have changed for only a few offenses (sex crimes especially), and even then just a little.[12] Third, when prosecutors seek a sentence of death, lay judge panels are actually *more likely* to impose the ultimate punishment than panels of three professional judges were in the old trial system. From 2010 to 2018, Japanese prosecutors sought a sentence of death for 53 defendants, and a death sentence was imposed on 36 of them (68 percent). By comparison, in the three decades that preceded the lay judge reform (1980–2009), prosecutors sought a sentence of death for 346 defendants, and a death sentence was imposed on 193 of them (56 percent).[13] Some of these signs of stasis in criminal justice outcomes result from adaptations to the lay judge system made by prosecutors and judges. Most notably, prosecutors have become more cautious about charging cases and seeking severe sentences, in order to avoid undesirable outcomes in a trial system that is unfamiliar and unpredictable.[14] The judiciary has been conservative too, especially in its

---

Domestic, Historical, and International Psychological Perspectives", *Vanderbilt Journal of Transnational Law*, Vol. 37 (2004), pp. 935–992.

[11] Takeda Masahiro, "Utagawashiki wa Muzai Tettei", *Fukui Shimbun*, March 10, 2019, p. 19.

[12] Stacey Steele, Carol Lawson, Mari Hirayama, and David T. Johnson, "Lay Participation in Japanese Criminal Justice: Prosecution Review Commissions, the Lay Judge System, and Penal Institution Visiting Committees", *Asian Journal of Law & Society* (forthcoming, 2020).

[13] Note, too, that the increased probability of a death sentence being imposed if prosecutors seek one partly reflects the fact that prosecutors have become more selective about seeking a sentence of death in the lay judge system. In the pre-reform period (1980–2009), prosecutors sought a sentence of death an average of 11.5 times per year. For the lay judge system (2010–2018), the comparable figure is 5.9. This decline in the number of death sentences sought not only reflects an increase in prosecutorial caution; it also reflects a decline in Japan's homicide rate. The increased propensity to impose a sentence of death when prosecutors seek one is especially noticeable in homicide cases with 3 or more victims. See Takeda Masahiro, "Genbatsuka no Ippo de Yuyo Oku", *Kyoto Shimbun*, March 23, 2019, p. 6.

[14] Takeda Masahiro, "Saibanin Seido Kaishi kara 5nen: Kensatsu wa Taisho Jiken o Shincho ni Kiso: Saibanin Kohosha no Jitairitsu, 60% Koeru", *Journalism*, September

reliance on benchmarks that are based on sentencing patterns from the pre-lay judge period.[15]

In sum, Japan's lay judge reform has stimulated change in formal rules and standard operating procedures in many parts of the criminal process, and the net effect could be a shift in the balance of power in Japanese criminal justice—a balance that long has favored law enforcement's interest in obtaining confessions, convictions, and capital sentences.[16] The lay judge reform has also stimulated more public interest and trust in Japanese criminal justice.[17] In these senses, the results of Japan's lay judge reform do seem "quite remarkable."[18] Yet there are also striking continuities in Japanese criminal justice, in conviction rates, in punishment patterns, and in death sentencing. Together they suggest that the changes in Japanese criminal procedure may be mostly incidental music. If the proof is in the pudding, then it needs to be acknowledged that Japan's lay judge system has not changed much that matters in criminal justice outcomes generally, or in capital punishment outcomes specifically—so far.[19] But the ripples of reform are continuing to spread. As the next section suggests, the future effects of the new trial system will depend on how judges and defense lawyers respond to prosecutors' efforts to maintain their control over case outcomes.[20]

2014, pp. 136–143; and Takeda Masahiro, "'Zaimei-Ochi' Hinpatsu Kisoritsu Teika", *Kochi Shimbun*, January 30, 2019, p. 12.

[15] Masahito Saeki and Eiichiro Watamura, "The Impact of Previous Sentencing Trends on Lay Judges' Sentencing Decisions," in Jianhong Liu and Setsuo Miyazawa, editors, *Crime and Justice in Contemporary Japan* (Springer, 2018), pp. 275–290.

[16] Malcolm M. Feeley and Setsuo Miyazawa, editors, *The Japanese Adversary System in Context: Controversies and Comparisons* (Palgrave Macmillan, 2002).

[17] See, for example, Masahiro Fujita, *Japanese Society and Lay Participation in Criminal Justice: Social Attitudes, Trust, and Mass Media* (Springer, 2018); and Ii Takayuki and Saibanin Raunji, editors, *Anata mo Ashita wa Saibanin!?* (Nihonhyoronsha, 2019).

[18] Daniel H. Foote, "Citizen Participation: Appraising the Saiban'in System", *Michigan State International Law Review*, Vol. 22, No. 3 (2014), p. 8.

[19] David T. Johnson, "Japan's Lay Judge System", in Jacqueline E. Ross and Stephen C. Thaman, editors, *Comparative Criminal Procedure* (Elgar, 2016), pp. 396–421.

[20] Takano Takashi, "Saibanin Seido no Koka: 10nen o Furikaette", *Jiyu to Seigi*, Vol. 70, No. 5 (May 2019), pp. 18–29.

Dogs That Do Not Bark

In Arthur Conan Doyle's "Silver Blaze" story (1892), detective Sherlock Holmes notices that a dog did not bark during the theft of a horse. From this, he induced that the thief was not a stranger, which reduced the number of suspects to one. Case closed.

> *Inspector Gregory of Scotland Yard*: You consider this to be important?
> *Sherlock Holmes*: Exceedingly so.
> *Inspector Gregory*: Is there any point to which you would wish to draw my attention?
> *Sherlock Holmes*: To the curious incident of the dog in the night-time.
> *Inspector Gregory*: The dog did nothing in the night-time.
> *Sherlock Holmes*: That was the curious incident.

The most curious thing about criminal justice reform in Japan is how much pressure for change has been directed at prosecutors—and how little has been directed at judges and defense lawyers. To be sure, prosecution does need reform. When more than one-quarter of prosecutors acknowledge that they have been directed by a superior to create a dossier (*chosho*) that differs from what a suspect or witness actually told them, the imperative of change is obvious.[21] It is also obvious that prosecutors and their allies will resist reform, for power seldom cedes control voluntarily.[22] But prosecutors are only one part of a "criminal court community" that is also inhabited by judges and defense lawyers. If prosecutors dominate this community, it is partly because judges and defense lawyers have let them. Much talk about reform overlooks the crucial fact that judges and defense lawyers have frequently failed to perform their duty to check prosecutors' power in the criminal process.[23]

Consider judges, who have the final word in the criminal process. They routinely use their authority to give prosecutors (and police) what they want: arrest warrants, detention warrants, evidence admitted at trial,

---

[21] *Asahi Shimbun*, "Kenji 26% 'Shiji Sareta Keiken': Jissai no Kyojutsu to Kotonaru Chosho no Sakusei," March 11, 2011, p. 38.

[22] Suo Masayuki, *Sore demo Boku wa Kaigi de Tatakau: Dokyumento Keiji Shiho Kaikaku* (Iwanami Shoten, 2015).

[23] David T. Johnson, *The Japanese Way of Justice: Prosecuting Crime in Japan* (Oxford University Press, 2002), pp. 61–85.

convictions, and sentences. And when prosecutors do not get what they want from lower courts, they frequently get it on appeal. There is nothing necessary or inevitable about this judicial tendency. Postwar reforms included many progressive provisions, from the right to due process and a fair trial to protection against self-incrimination. But in translating the "law on the books" into the "law in action," Japan's judiciary has "adopted, accepted, or silently acquiesced in a wide range of interpretations that greatly circumscribed the protections for suspects and defendants, while granting broad authority to investigators."[24] This extraordinary deference of judges to prosecutors is why some defense lawyers say that if they could change only one thing about Japanese criminal justice, it would be the tendency of judges to yield to prosecutors in their decision-making. On this view, judges defer to prosecutors so routinely that reforming the judiciary is even more urgent than reforming the procuracy. As one defense lawyer put it, "if judges change, prosecutors will have to change too."[25]

Like judges, defense lawyers have also been passive toward prosecutors and police. Legally and ethically, their obligation is to try, by every fair and legal means, to get the best result for their clients, but this duty often goes unfulfilled. For decades, many defense lawyers have been little more than passive props in trial ceremonies that are scripted by prosecutors, certified by judges, and barely contested by the defense. There are many reasons for this passivity, including some over which defense lawyers have little control. Judicial interpretations of law have restricted what defense attorneys can do for criminal suspects and defendants. Moreover, all but a few criminal cases pay poorly in comparison to the other work opportunities that Japanese attorneys have (in criminal defense as in other areas of life, you often get what you pay for). But while law and economics are impediments to good defense lawyering in Japan, the cultural obstacles may be even more formidable. In my view, defense lawyers are complicit in a state of affairs that Hirano Ryuichi (former president of Tokyo University and the dean of criminal justice studies in Japan) described as "abnormal," "diseased," and "really quite

---

[24] Daniel H. Foote, "Policymaking by the Japanese Judiciary in the Criminal Justice Field," *Hoshakaigaku*, No. 72 (2010), p. 18.

[25] David T. Johnson, "War in a Season of Slow Revolution: Defense Lawyers and Lay Judges in Japanese Criminal Justice", *The Asia-Pacific Journal/Japan Focus*, Vol. 9 (June 29, 2011), pp. 1–11.

hopeless."[26] Traditionally, defense lawyers in Japan have seldom advised suspects or defendants to invoke their right to silence. In 1991, a survey of more than 1000 lawyers found that over 60 percent had never recommended that a suspect or defendant exercise the right to remain silent. *Not a single time*. The same survey found that two-thirds of lawyers had never asked that a witness testifies in court when prosecutors sought to use written statements instead of live testimony, and three-quarters had never asked a court to compel prosecutors to disclose evidence. This level of passive acquiescence is like doing *sumo* with one hand tied behind your back.

Since it is often in a suspect's best interest not to talk to interrogators, it is puzzling why there is so much reluctance to recommend this fundamental right. One cause is the difficulty of maintaining silence through Japan's long interrogation process. As one attorney told me, "if I advise 100 suspects to remain silent, only one or two would be capable of staying mute until the [long] interrogations end."[27] Still, in many criminal cases the best thing a defendant in Japan can do is what a full-page ad in the Boston Yellow Pages once urged (under "Attorneys"): JUST SHUT UP.

Even in trials where defendants claim innocence, it is striking how little vigorous advocacy there can be. During a rape trial in which the defendant insisted that the victim had consented to sex, I watched one defense lawyer scold his client in open court. "Who are you trying to kid?" he asked his befuddled client. "Do you really think anyone is going to believe your story? I don't." And in a murder trial in which prosecutors sought a sentence of death for a defendant who had a prior conviction for homicide, a pair of defense lawyers passed up numerous opportunities to press the prosecution's key witnesses about weaknesses in their testimony. When prosecutors in this trial persistently pressed the defendant with incriminating questions despite the defendant's complete silence, his lawyers barely uttered a word of protest. I was not surprised when that defendant was condemned to death. And I suppose he may have wondered about his own legal representation: with friends like this, who needs enemies?

---

[26] Hirano Ryuichi, "Diagnosis of the Current Code of Criminal Procedure", *Law in Japan*, Vol. 22 (1989), pp. 129–142.

[27] David T. Johnson, "War in a Season of Slow Revolution: Defense Lawyers and Lay Judges in Japanese Criminal Justice", *The Asia-Pacific Journal/Japan Focus*, Vol. 9 (June 29, 2011), pp. 1–11.

It is difficult to defend homicide cases in a country where the criminal process is significantly tilted toward state interests. It also needs to be acknowledged that there is not one right way to do criminal defense. Culture counts, and in Japan's legal culture, repentance and confession are salient themes.[28] Criminal defense strategy should depend on the case and the context—and Japan is not the United States. But sometimes the best defense is a good offense, even in Japan.

Defending someone accused of murder is not a job for people seeking approval. It is a job for those who are willing to rattle cages, make enemies, and raise a little hell. By raising hell, defense lawyers honor the law.[29] The need to "rattle cages" is what defense lawyer Takano Takashi had in mind when he told me that the lay judge system gives Japanese defense lawyers a precious opportunity to improve a system that sorely needs change:

> The advent of the lay judge system [in 2009] marks the beginning of a war against professional judges. Many professional judges want to minimize the scope and significance of the lay judge reform. But this is a power struggle. [If we are to fulfill our obligation to protect the rights of defendants,] we defense lawyers must empower lay judges to stand up to professional judges and defeat them in the deliberation room. For this to happen, defense lawyers must shed the feeling of uselessness that has been their big burden. Defense lawyers are habituated to being passive in the criminal process. We have been socialized to believe that what we do does not matter. But with lay judges in front of us, we are no longer talking to a wall. Now we have a real opportunity to make a difference, and we need to make the most of it. We must fight in open court to change a system that is stacked against us.[30]

Time will tell what Japanese defense lawyers make of the new opportunities the lay judge reform is giving them. By most accounts, defense lawyering has improved since the reform took effect in 2009. At the same time, lay judges routinely report that they found the trial

---

[28] Daniel H. Foote, "The Benevolent Paternalism of Japanese Criminal Justice", *California Law Review*, Vol. 80, No. 2 (1992), pp. 317–390.

[29] Alan Dershowitz, *The Best Defense* (Vintage, 1983).

[30] David T. Johnson, "War in a Season of Slow Revolution: Defense Lawyers and Lay Judges in Japanese Criminal Justice", *The Asia-Pacific Journal/Japan Focus*, Vol. 9 (June 29, 2011), pp. 1–11.

presentations made by prosecutors clearer and more persuasive than those made by defense lawyers.[31] And continued change for the better in Japanese defense lawyering is far from guaranteed, not least because of new challenges raised by the other major reform in civilian participation in Japan's criminal process.

VICTIMS AND THE MYTH OF CLOSURE

The second major reform in Japanese criminal justice is the creation of a victim participation system that moves victims and survivors close to center stage of the criminal process. One question is whether the increased salience of victims in Japanese capital punishment constitutes progress or regress. The answer depends on whether one regards capital punishment as a victim-service program.[32]

Victims have long been neglected and ignored in Japan's criminal process, and they certainly deserve more support and consideration than they have historically received. But while efforts to help them are necessary, Japan's victims' rights movement has been, for the most part, harshly punitive. Other models for thinking about how victims might be helped have been neglected and ignored, including some that are more "restorative" in the sense that they focus on healing the harms caused by crime rather than encouraging the venting of vengeful feelings.[33]

In Japan's punitive approach to victims' rights, victims and their families have taken on an almost sacred status in the criminal process, and this makes it difficult to cross-examine them or otherwise challenge their assertions.[34] Since vigorous cross-examination is an indispensable tool for determining truth at trial, the difficulty of using it with victims and survivors is worrisome. In a murder trial in Tokyo, for example, the victim's

---

[31] Erik Herber, *Lay and Expert Contributions to Japanese Criminal Justice* (Routledge, 2019), p. 172.

[32] David T. Johnson, "Killing Asahara: What Japan Can Learn About Victims and Capital Punishment from the Execution of an American Terrorist", *The Asia-Pacific Journal/Japan Focus*, Vol. 10 (September 9, 2012), pp. 1–15.

[33] Danielle Sered, *Until We Reckon: Violence, Mass Incarceration, and a Road to Repair* (The New Press, 2019).

[34] Maiko Tagusari, "Does the Death Penalty Serve Victims?"; and David T. Johnson, "Does Capital Punishment Bring Closure to Victims?", in Ivan Simonovic, editor, *Death Penalty and the Victims* (United Nations, 2016), pp. 41–48 and pp. 75–82.

mother testified that she missed her deceased daughter greatly even though (the defense lawyer knew) the mother and daughter had been on bad terms for years before the daughter was killed, and even though the mother collected a tidy life insurance sum after the loss of her daughter. The defense lawyer told me that he remained silent about this issue out of fear of being criticized for "re-victimizing" the mother. When victims are seen as sacred, some truths are hard to utter.

Many supporters of capital punishment believe death sentences and executions give victims "closure"—a satisfying feeling that something terrible has ended. But closure of this kind is a myth, for survivors are never "over and done with" their loss. The unfortunate truth is that their suffering does not end. A better conception of closure would see it as a process of "memory work" through which survivors construct meaningful narratives about a killing and how they have dealt with it. In this sense, the quest for closure continues for as long as the survivor is alive, and recognizing the myth of closure reminds survivors that they should not hope for a finality that is illusory. The promise of closure as an ending is a false comfort that is doomed to disappoint.[35]

Capital punishment seldom provides closure for persons bereaved by homicide, but it does create resentment among those whose cases are not deemed capital. In Japan, prosecutors seek a sentence of death in only about 1 out of every 100–200 murder cases. When the severity of a sentence is regarded as a measure of how much a victim is valued—and when a death sentence is seen as a token of society's esteem for a victim—the non-capital sentences that most defendants receive foster the perception among survivors that the victim they have lost is undervalued.[36] To dispel this perception, prosecutors would need to seek capital sanctions as frequently as they were used in the Tokugawa era. Even the most ardent supporters of Japanese capital punishment do not want to go back to that future.

While closure is mostly a myth, it is a myth that performs important functions in the age of abolition. For one thing, closure paints over the disturbing reality of execution with a positive patina that people can endorse, for it is easier to say (and to be seen as saying) "I support

---

[35] Jody Lynee Madeira, *Killing McVeigh: The Death Penalty and the Myth of Closure* (New York University Press, 2012).

[36] Scott Turow, *Ultimate Punishment: A Lawyer's Reflections on Dealing with the Death Penalty* (Farrar, Straus and Giroux, 2003), pp. 47–56.

victims" than "I want vengeance." For another, when closure is a central purpose of capital punishment, people do not need to worry about whether execution is an excessive use of power by government, because the closure frame "de-governmentalizes" the death penalty by depicting the state as the servant of society rather than its master. The language of "closure" also connects capital punishment to the history of community control over punishment. In the United States, claims about closure are linked to bloody traditions of lynching and vigilantism. In Japan, the language of closure is connected to a rhetoric of "repentance" and "atonement" that has been salient for centuries. The essence of this rhetoric is: "I want the offender to repent and atone; I want him dead." It is no coincidence that the rise of closure and its cognates corresponded with death penalty increases in Japan after 2000 and with death penalty increases in the United States a decade earlier. When the death penalty is framed as a matter of serving victims and helping them achieve closure, the ultimate effect is the legitimation of a sanction that has become increasingly difficult to justify on other grounds.[37]

VICTIMS AND THE CULTURE OF VENGEANCE

Murder trials in Japan are emotionally intense. Tears are everywhere. Survivors cry when they testify and while observing the proceedings. Spectators and reporters weep. Prosecutors cry when they describe the suffering of the survivors. Defense lawyers cry while listening to the statements of the bereaved. Defendants cry—and when they are not crying they slump over in postures of anguish and shame. And the defendant's parents and relatives often cry while reading their statements to the court. One mother of a defendant asked the court for permission to apologize to the survivors. When it was granted, she turned to face them and said—while bowing 90 degrees and sobbing uncontrollably—"I am extremely sorry for what my son has done and for what you have had to go through" (at which point I had to wipe my own eyes). One of the judges cried as this mother spoke, and four of the lay judges also cried during this trial—two of them openly and often. These tears at trial

---

[37] Franklin E. Zimring, *The Contradictions of American Capital Punishment* (Oxford University Press, 2003), pp. 42–66.

express a wide range of emotions, from sadness, sorrow, and regret to anguish, anger, and rage.[38]

While emotions are a fact of life, it is difficult to discern their proper role in a criminal trial. In 1977 the U.S. Supreme Court held that "it is of vital importance to the defendant and to the community that any decision to impose the death sentence be, and appear to be, based on reason" (*Gardner v. Florida*). More broadly, one theme of American jurisprudence since the 1970s has been the effort to "rationalize" the sentencing process, which requires the substitution of rational principles and rule-of-law values for punitive passions and unguided jury discretion. But ironically, the U.S. Supreme Court also permits prosecutors to present "victim impact" evidence in the penalty phase of capital trials (though in America victims are not allowed to make specific sentencing requests such as "I demand a death sentence"). It is hard to imagine a rule that is more contrary to the Court's rationalizing reforms.[39]

In Japan, the victim participation system permits the family and friends of homicide victims to lobby for death penalty outcomes, which they frequently do. But allowing the bereaved to beg for a capital sentence can distort the court's deliberations and the prosecutors' decision about whether to seek a death sentence in the first place. In one murder trial, a parade of two surviving parents, their attorney, four victims, and two prosecutors spent more than three hours of the final trial session begging for the defendant to be given the death sentence that he eventually received. In another, the sister of a murder victim started her testimony by stating that she "hates" the defendant, and the longer she spoke the more passionate she became. She sobbed while reading her statement, and she emphasized how "vexed" she felt by the defendant's "evil acts." She even rebuked the defendant for trying to "trick" the court in his testimony. "You merely said what was convenient for you," she insisted. "Give us the lives of our loved ones back!" Near the end of her statement she broke into gasping sobs and, when she could not continue, someone stepped forward to finish reading it to the lay judge panel. The final words were as follows:

---

[38] David T. Johnson, "Capital Punishment Without Capital Trials in Japan's Lay Judge System", *The Asia-Pacific Journal/Japan Focus*, Vol. 7 (2009), p. 7.

[39] David Garland, *Peculiar Institution: America's Death Penalty in an Age of Abolition* (The Belknap Press of Harvard University Press, 2010), p. 279.

I went to visit my sister's grave the other day, and I told her that the next time I come I will definitely bring news of a death sentence. My beloved sister is watching this trial, and I really want the court to give us a death sentence. I desire a death sentence. I hope you will do as I request.[40]

Japanese officials often justify capital punishment in terms of retribution, but retribution can be the victim's vengeance in disguise. Moreover, proponents of capital punishment often hide behind victims by identifying with their wrath, because this is a more comfortable expression of their own feelings than a direct statement would be. This kind of hiding is especially common among prosecutors, who claim they want to serve survivors when the latter's preferences align with their own, but who ignore survivors' preferences when they point in a different (non-capital) direction. Some prosecutors also fail to serve the bereaved by neglecting to inform them that a capital sentence will probably result in prolonged litigation before an execution can occur. A sense of an ending is unlikely to come for years or even decades. In some respects this is how it should be, for in the administration of capital punishment, the quick is the enemy of the careful.

Decisions about the death penalty are too important to be made by or for survivors. In a democracy, no minority, even those whose tragedies burn our hearts, should be empowered to speak for everyone.[41] It is difficult to discern the proper role for citizens' preferences in structuring the governance of punishment in democratic systems. The preferences of victims and survivors may be relevant, but they must not be allowed to marginalize other practical and jurisprudential considerations. Too often, though, the feelings of survivors are presented as trump cards that should take precedence over everything else.

At present, the hunger of victims for revenge remains one of the least discussed but most pervasive forces in Japanese capital punishment. Because Japanese law does not recognize that death is different, it provides little protection against the powerful push of survivors' anger and anguish. And because of the central role that emotions play in Japanese murder trials, it is imperative to create a two-stage system of trial that

---

[40] David T. Johnson, "Capital Punishment Without Capital Trials in Japan's Lay Judge System", *The Asia-Pacific Journal/Japan Focus*, Vol. 7 (2009), p. 6.

[41] Scott Turow, *Ultimate Punishment: A Lawyer's Reflections on Dealing with the Death Penalty* (Farrar, Straus and Giroux, 2003), p. 56.

separates guilt-determination from sentence-determination. This is especially urgent when a defendant pleads not guilty, for research shows that the probability of a criminal conviction increases when judges and jurors hear victim testimony ("The defendant must atone with his life!") that is unrelated to the question of guilt.[42]

The death penalty is often an act of revenge, and vengeance is not a principled justification for the ultimate punishment; it is a violent emotion that insists on its own righteousness. It is, therefore, dangerous—not least to the person who feeds it. As sages have cautioned for centuries, "Before you embark on a journey of revenge, dig two graves."

Entrenchment or Change?

The number of countries to abolish capital punishment has increased remarkably in recent years. One cause of this surge in abolition is the emergence of a "human rights dynamic" that recognizes capital punishment as a denial of the universal human rights to life and to freedom from cruel and inhuman punishment.[43] The fate of capital punishment in countries that retain it will be shaped by the ongoing battle between two competing frames. Is the death penalty a matter of human rights? Or is it a victim service program?

During the last decade, victims have acquired more influence in Japanese murder trials and in the pretrial and appellate processes. The result is that Japanese capital punishment is shaped by a culture of vengeance. In this culture, vengeance is both an individual victim's emotional reaction to loss and a form of public anger. In both forms, vengeance insists on its own righteousness—no matter what.[44] Because of this self-righteous certainty, vengeance has little regard for factual or moral complexity. Vengeance also promises a catharsis that cannot come through capital punishment (only the attachments that people have to each other can provide some sense of relief). And vengeance is undemocratic when it privileges the emotions of a handful

---

[42] Itoh Yuji, *Saibanin no Handan no Shinri: Shinrigaku Jikken kara Semaru* (Keio Gijuku Mitatetsu Gakkai, 2019), pp. 48–66.

[43] Roger Hood and Carolyn Hoyle, "Abolishing the Death Penalty Worldwide: The Impact of a 'New Dynamic'", *Crime and Justice*, Vol. 38, No. 1 (2009), pp. 1–63.

[44] Terry K. Aladjem, *The Culture of Vengeance and the Fate of American Justice* (Cambridge University Press, 2008).

of people. In thinking about capital punishment in the Japanese future, the tradeoff is not between "concern for victims" and some misplaced "compassion for offenders" (as many observers suppose). It is between vengeance and human rights.

Japan's culture of vengeance can be resisted. One recourse is a more skeptical awareness of the disutility of anger in deciding criminal punishments. Another is a willingness to buck the tides of popular sentiment—an openness to doubting what others see as moral and factual certainties. But above all, challenging Japan's culture of vengeance requires recognizing that vengeance is a kind of "wild justice": the more people run to it, the more law ought to weed it out.[45] All of these forms of resistance presuppose personal and political courage. They will not be easy. But as Aristotle observed, courage is the first of human virtues because it makes all of the others possible. Without the courage that enables resistance to Japan's culture of vengeance, the victim participation system could entrench capital punishment more deeply into Japanese law and society.

As for Japan's lay judge reform, the future effects of this form of citizen participation are difficult to discern. On the one hand, it is widely considered imperative not to "burden" (*futan*) lay judges unduly. Indeed, Japanese judges, journalists, and citizens are so concerned about the physical and emotional "burdens" purportedly imposed on lay judges that this secondary objective threatens to displace core aims of criminal justice, such as fairness, justice, and accuracy. The preoccupation with the well-being of lay judges can be seen in newspaper headlines such as these: Extreme Burden for Lay Judges (*Nikkei*); The Psychological Fatigue of Lay Judges (*Mainichi*); Lay Judge Duty Takes a Heavy Toll (*Yomiuri*); and An Appeal to Care for the Hearts of Lay Judges (*Asahi*). The central premise of any system of capital justice is that the ultimate punishment must be administered in a manner that is fair, just, and accurate. This is partly a question of *factual accuracy*—whether the defendant actually committed the crime for which he or she has been charged. But even if a system of justice were able to eliminate the possibility of sentencing an innocent person to death (and this is *not* possible, as explained in Chapter 4), another crucial question concerns the *moral accuracy* of death penalty decisions. Capital punishment ought to be administered in a manner that is both

---

[45] Susan Jacoby, *Wild Justice: The Evolution of Revenge* (Harper & Row, 1983).

consistent (treating like cases alike) and individualized (treating different cases differently). And capital punishment must also be administered based on a careful consideration of each defendant's culpability, not on morally irrelevant factors such as class, the intensity of a victim's anger, or judicial and public convenience. In Japan, factual and moral accuracy are being threatened by a jurisprudence which assumes that death is not different, and by the reluctance of judges to deviate from a pre-established trial script that has been designed to minimize the "burdens" imposed on lay judges. An excessive concern with the emotional well-being of lay judges creates perverse incentives because it encourages judges to cut corners in the criminal process in order to protect the valuable time and vulnerable psyches of their lay colleagues on the bench—and in order to protect themselves from criticism, too. One analyst believes the end result of this misplaced focus will be a "dead culture of law" in which core criminal justice values are subordinated to the tertiary concerns of convenience and efficiency.[46] More broadly, the presence of lay judges in Japan conveys the impression that the public is making life-and-death decisions when in fact state officials—prosecutors and judges especially—are still the voices that matter most. The perception that "the people" are doing it may bolster the legitimacy of capital punishment and make it more resistant to reform and repeal.

On the other hand, the full effects of legal reform will take many years to realize.[47] If the lay judge reform is "a stone into the pond" of Japan's criminal process, its' ripples could slowly transform capital punishment by insisting that state killing is not just state business—it is the business of civil society too. The fresh eyes of society are important because, in law as in life, the more one looks at a thing, the less one sees it. As the English writer G. K. Chesterton observed a century ago:

> It is a terrible business to mark a man out for the vengeance of men. But it is a thing to which a man can grow accustomed, as he can to other terrible things…The horrible thing about all legal officials—even the best—about

---

[46] Takano Takashi, "Saibanin Seido no Koka: 10nen o Furikaette", *Jiyu to Seigi*, Vol. 70, No. 5 (May 2019), pp. 26–29.

[47] David T. Johnson and Setsuo Miyazawa, "Japanese Court Reform on Trial", in Rosann Greenspan, Hadar Aviram, and Jonathan Simon, editors, *The Legal Process and the Promise of Justice: Studies Inspired by the Work of Malcolm Feeley* (Cambridge University Press, 2019), pp. 122–138.

all judges, magistrates, barristers, detectives, and policemen, is not that they are wicked (some of them are good), and not that they are stupid (several of them are quite intelligent). It is simply that they have got used to it. Strictly, they do not see the prisoner in the dock; all they see is the usual man in the usual place. They do not see the awful court of judgment; they only see their own workshop.[48]

Many Japanese judges have "got used to" presuming that "the usual man in the usual place" deserves (more or less) the punishment that prosecutors propose.[49] A conviction rate close to 100 percent testifies to this terrible tendency, and so does a *Mainichi* newspaper survey (March 9, 2011) which found that not a single prosecutor (out of 40) believed Japan's high conviction rate reflects problems in the judiciary. Defense lawyers have also grown "used to" being passive in the criminal process. Many seem not to appreciate how terrible "the awful court of judgment" can be for the person being judged. For criminal defendants, the right to an attorney is the most fundamental right because it is the one that makes all other rights meaningful. If defense lawyers fail to seize the opportunities afforded by the lay judge reform, it will likely end in disappointment. Rights are rarely bequeathed by benevolent authorities; they emerge out of experience with injustice, and getting them recognized requires that defense lawyers raise a little hell. If the ripples of the lay judge reform do continue to spread, then the common sense of citizens could help correct the tendency of judges to see "the awful court of judgment" as their own familiar workshop—and defense lawyers may realize they are no longer "talking to a wall." This, anyway, is a scenario for the future that recognizes potential for change in Japanese capital punishment through the mechanism of citizen participation. Time will tell more. The final chapter of this book explores how public opinion and politics could shape Japanese capital punishment in the years to come.

---

[48] G. K. Chesterton, "The Twelve Men," in *Tremendous Trifles* (1909).
[49] Segi Hiroshi, *Zetsubo no Saibansho* (Kodansha Gendai Shinsho, 2014).

Open Access This chapter is licensed under the terms of the Creative Commons Attribution-NonCommercial-NoDerivatives 4.0 International License (http://creativecommons.org/licenses/by-nc-nd/4.0/), which permits any noncommercial use, sharing, distribution and reproduction in any medium or format, as long as you give appropriate credit to the original author(s) and the source, provide a link to the Creative Commons license and indicate if you modified the licensed material. You do not have permission under this license to share adapted material derived from this chapter or parts of it.

The images or other third party material in this chapter are included in the chapter's Creative Commons license, unless indicated otherwise in a credit line to the material. If material is not included in the chapter's Creative Commons license and your intended use is not permitted by statutory regulation or exceeds the permitted use, you will need to obtain permission directly from the copyright holder.

CHAPTER 6

The Death Penalty and Democracy

Abstract Many people in Japan argue that for abolition or significant death penalty reform to occur, public discussion (*giron*) must first change public opinion. This belief is misleading, because public opinion about capital punishment in Japan is rooted in moral intuitions about retribution and atonement that are largely impervious to rational discussion, and because death penalty abolitions and moratoria are invariably caused by political leadership from the front, not by changes in public perception. Claims that capital punishment reflects "democracy-at-work" are similarly simplistic because "democracy" means more than majority rule. If the abolition of capital punishment does occur in Japan, it will probably have several positive consequences for Japanese criminal justice and society.

Keywords Public opinion · Chiba Keiko · Marshall hypothesis · Leadership from the front · Article 9 · Representative democracy · Participatory democracy · Legal democracy · Liberal democracy

Why would an abolitionist Minister of Justice order executions? Chiba Keiko was the first of eight people to serve as Minister of Justice while the Democratic Party of Japan controlled Japan's central government between August 2009 and December 2012. She held the post for one year, and she was one of three DPJ Ministers to authorize executions. In

© The Author(s) 2020
D. T. Johnson, *The Culture of Capital Punishment in Japan*,
Palgrave Advances in Criminology and Criminal Justice in Asia,
https://doi.org/10.1007/978-3-030-32086-7_6

July 2010, she ordered the hanging of two men, Shinozawa Kazuo, who was convicted of killing six persons, and Ogata Hidenori, who was convicted of killing two. In addition to signing their death warrants, Chiba attended their hangings at the gallows in Tokyo, something no modern Minister had done, and she permitted a few select journalists to view the Tokyo gallows when not in operation—a sharp break from the customary secrecy that shrouds executions in Japan. Then Chiba established a "Study Group about the State of Capital Punishment" in her Ministry of Justice, which released a report of its findings in March 2012 that included little information about the reality of execution.

These actions by Chiba—particularly the executions she ordered—attracted much attention, especially from fellow abolitionists, many of whom believe she betrayed the cause of abolition. Some of her critics—lawyers, politicians, and members of NGOs—expressed anger and dismay. In their view, Chiba accomplished nothing positive by ordering the executions, she violated her own beliefs about human rights and the sanctity of life, she greased the wheels of the machinery of death for her DPJ successors (two of whom would authorize executions in 2012), and she set back the cause of death penalty reform, which the DPJ said it was committed to in the campaign that culminated in its landslide victory in the summer 2009 election.

In 2016, Chiba provided her most detailed explanation for the executions that she ordered.[1] It is the third explanation she has given, and it is the clearest. In the previous two explanations—an essay in the *Asahi* newspaper, and an interview in an NHK documentary—Chiba's words reminded me of George Orwell's observation that "The great enemy of clear language is insincerity."[2] I do not know why Chiba's third account is clearer, but I have two hunches. For one, repetition sometimes improves the clarity of an explanation (ask a teacher or preacher). For another, Horikawa Keiko, who conducted the interview of Chiba in 2016, is a master journalist who possesses a knack for telling interesting stories. Whatever the reasons, Chiba should be commended for (finally)

---

[1] Chiba Keiko, interviewed by Horikawa Keiko, "'Naze Shikko' no Toi o Kakaete" ["Engaging the Question of 'Why I Executed'"], *Sekai*, March 2016, pp. 160–170.

[2] Chiba Keiko, "*Shikko no Shomei wa Watashi Narino Koishi: Shikei - Nayami Fukaki Mori*", *Asahi Shimbun*, November 20, 2010; and "*Shikei Shikko: Homu Daijin no Kunou*" (NHK ETV Tokushu, broadcast on February 27, 2011).

explaining why she authorized the hangings in 2010. She could have hidden behind silence and platitudes, as most Ministers of Justice do when it comes to capital punishment, and as most prosecutors and politicians do too. Here is what we learn from her interview with Horikawa.

1. Chiba's main reason for authorizing the executions in 2010 was to stimulate "public discussion" (*giron*) about capital punishment in Japan.
2. Chiba planned to authorize executions from the moment she accepted the Minister of Justice job in September 2009, some ten months before the hangings occurred.
3. Chiba does not believe the executions she authorized actually advanced public discussion.
4. Chiba does not believe the executions served victims or the cause of justice.
5. Officials in the Ministry of Justice did not pressure Chiba to sign the death warrants.
6. Chiba believes many officials in the Ministry of Justice oppose capital punishment or feel ambivalent about it.
7. Before the 2010 executions, Chiba asked officials in the Ministry for information about the reality of hanging, but they refused to give it to her.
8. Ministry of Justice officials did not try to dissuade Chiba from attending the two hangings she authorized.
9. The executions Chiba observed were so "cruel" and "hideous" that she finds them difficult to describe.
10. Chiba believes Japan is slowly moving toward the abolition of capital punishment.

All of these assertions are interesting, but I shall focus on the first, for Chiba's belief that executions would promote "public discussion" (*giron*) about capital punishment is surely the main point of her interview. Indeed, the term "public discussion" occurs 29 times in its 11 pages. The frequent repetition of this expression and its appearance in key parts of the text (including the subtitle of the article and the first section heading) reflects Chiba's core conviction that for significant death penalty reform to occur, public discussion must first change public opinion.

This belief is widely shared in Japan,³ but it is misleading in at least three ways, as the following section shows.⁴

On Public Opinion and Capital Punishment

First, more than 140 countries have abolished the death penalty in law or have gone more than ten years in a row without an execution, yet in none of these countries did the change result from majority public opinion pushing for reform. There are few iron laws in socio-legal studies, but this may be one: when executions cease or the death penalty disappears, the primary proximate cause is leadership by political elites, despite public support for capital punishment at the time of the reform.⁵ This pattern of "leadership from the front" suggests that efforts to convince a majority of Japanese people to oppose capital punishment are probably doomed to fail. In this sense, public education campaigns are a hollow hope—though of course they are not irrelevant. Their primary value is their influence on the views of elite decision-makers, who are the actors with the practical ability to secure abolition or a moratorium. Still, the main lesson from the rest of the world is that "the straightest road to abolition" often involves "bypassing public opinion entirely."⁶ A parallel lesson can be learned from Japan's closest cousins, South Korea and Taiwan, both of which have experienced moratoria on executions in recent years (Taiwan from 2006 through 2009, and South Korea from 1998 to the present). In both countries, the cessation of executions had "little to do with public opinion, which generally favors retaining the death penalty."⁷ Executions ceased primarily because political leaders wanted to stop this form of state killing.

---

³See, for example, Sato Mai, "Yoron to Iu Shinwa: Nozomu no wa 'Shikei' Desu ka", *Sekai*, March 2016, pp. 183–191.

⁴See also David T. Johnson, "Shikei no 'Giron' e no Gimon: Chiba moto Homu Daijin e no Intabyu o Megutte" [on the Interview of Former Minister of Justice Chiba Keiko in the March 2016 Issue of *Sekai*], *Sekai*, No. 882 (May 2016), pp. 228–235 (translated by Naoko Iwakawa and Makoto Ibusuki).

⁵Franklin E. Zimring, *The Contradictions of American Capital Punishment* (Oxford University Press, 2003), pp. 17–26.

⁶Andrew Hammel, *Ending the Death Penalty: The European Experience in Global Perspective* (Palgrave Macmillan, 2010), p. 236.

⁷Sangmin Bae, "International Norms, Domestic Politics, and the Death Penalty: Comparing Japan, South Korea, and Taiwan", *Comparative Politics*, Vol. 44, No. 1, p. 41.

A second stubborn fact is that public support for capital punishment in Japan is rooted in sentiments about retribution and atonement.[8] As a result, the belief that death is deserved for certain heinous offenders is more a matter of emotion and intuition than reason or evidence. In this context, providing more information about capital punishment is unlikely to alter habits of the heart, for humans are adept at ignoring contrary evidence and discounting or denying its significance.[9] On hot-button issues such as capital punishment and immigration, facts can even be counter-productive, for research shows that the smarter a person is, the greater his or her ability to rationalize discordant information.[10] When people take the trouble to think about capital punishment at all, they often engage in post hoc justification, which tends to reinforce their bedrock beliefs in retribution and atonement.

Third, changing public opinion about capital punishment is always difficult and sometimes impossible. In a 1972 decision (*Furman v. Georgia*), U.S. Supreme Court Justice Thurgood Marshall famously stressed the importance of public opinion in settling questions about the constitutionality of capital punishment under the "cruel and unusual" clause of the Eighth Amendment. Justice Marshall made three connected claims: (a) most Americans lack knowledge about capital punishment; (b) the more Americans learn about capital punishment, the less they will support it; and (c) commitments to capital punishment that are rooted in retribution are especially difficult to change. In a subsequent death penalty opinion (*Gregg v. Georgia* in 1976), Justice Marshall stated that if the American people were better informed about capital punishment, "they would find it shocking, unjust, and unacceptable." In his view, the key question about capital punishment is not whether

---

[8] See, for example, Mari Kita and David T. Johnson, "Framing Capital Punishment in Japan: Avoidance, Ambivalence, and Atonement", *Asian Journal of Criminology*, Vol. 9, No. 3 (September 2014), pp. 221–240. See also Mai Sato, *The Death Penalty in Japan: Will the Public Tolerate Abolition?* (Springer VS, 2014); and Hamai Koichi's book review in *Social Science Japan Journal* (January 2015), pp. 103–106 (arguing that "there is an extremely deep-rooted belief in Japan that criminals should receive heavy penalties").

[9] Jonathan Haidt, *The Righteous Mind: Why Good People Are Divided by Politics and Religion* (Pantheon, 2012).

[10] Tali Sharot, *The Influential Mind: What the Brain Reveals About Our Power to Change Others* (Henry Holt, 2017).

"a substantial proportion of American citizens would today, if polled, opine that [it] is barbarously cruel, but whether they would find it to be so in light of *all information presently available*" (emphasis added). The Marshall Hypothesis (as it came to be called) has been the subject of much study, and results are "decidedly mixed."[11] In some studies of American attitudes, more information about capital punishment does not lead to more distaste for it. In other studies, information alters opinion for a while, but opinion eventually rebounds back to its original position. In still other studies, information persuades some people to become more opposed to capital punishment while persuading others to become more supportive of it. Research has also been done to explore the relevance of the Marshall hypothesis in Japan. In one study, when Japanese citizens were given information about capital punishment and allowed to deliberate with other people about the issue, 11 out of 50 participants shifted their support from retention to abolition, while 9 of the 50 changed their attitude in the opposite direction.[12] More research is needed, but this finding suggests that "public discussion" (*giron*) may do little to alter overall support for capital punishment.

Before Japan's lay judge reform took effect in 2009, some analysts predicted that the new trial system would result in fewer death sentences, because citizens on lay judge panels would be forced to think deeply about the death penalty, and because (some prognosticators supposed) the harder citizens thought about it, the more reluctant they would be to support it.[13] As explained in Chapter 5, this has not happened. In fact, since 2009, lay judge panels have actually been substantially more likely to impose a sentence of death when prosecutors seek one than panels of three professional judges were in the homicide trial system that operated until 2009.[14] The Marshall hypothesis also receives little

---

[11] Carol Steiker, "The Marshall Hypothesis Revisited", *Howard Law Journal* (2009), pp. 525–558.

[12] Mai Sato, *The Death Penalty in Japan: Will the Public Tolerate Abolition?* (Springer VS, 2014), pp. 157–180.

[13] Leah Ambler, "The People Decide: The Effect of the Introduction of the Quasi-Jury System (*Saiban-in Seido*) on the Death Penalty in Japan", *Northwestern Journal of International Human Rights*, Vol. 6, No. 1 (Fall 2008), pp. 1–23.

[14] Takeda Masahiro, "Genbatsuka no Ippo de Yuyo Oku", *Kyoto Shimbun*, March 23, 2019, p. 6.

support in America, where 80 percent of the citizens who serve as capital jurors do not change their mind about capital punishment, and where those who do change their mind are actually more likely to become more supportive of capital punishment than to become more opposed to it. In short, there is little empirical support for the premise about "public discussion" (*giron*) that motivated Minister of Justice Chiba Keiko to order executions in the summer of 2010.

Ironically, the strongest support for the Marshall hypothesis is found among the judges on the U.S. Supreme Court where Justice Thurgood Marshall served. Several American Justices who started their careers on the U.S. Supreme Court supporting capital punishment converted to anti-death penalty views after serving many years and considering many capital appeals.[15] Most notably, Justices Lewis Powell, John Paul Stevens, and Potter Stewart voted in favor of capital punishment in a 1976 case (*Gregg v. Georgia*) that helped restart America's machinery of death after the country had gone nearly ten years without an execution. By the end of their tenures on the bench—after many years of applying the American jurisprudence of "super due process" and after the discovery of "capital error" in numerous death penalty cases—all three came to conclude that it is impossible to administer the death penalty in a manner that is consistent with the protections promised by American law. As Justice Powell remarked after his retirement, whatever attractions capital punishment might have in principle, its actual practice "serves no useful purpose and brings discredit on the whole legal system."[16] Other Justices on the U.S. Supreme Court have learned a similar lesson: to love the law is to hate capital punishment.[17] Indeed, the growing recognition that supports for capital punishment is inconsistent with respect for law has led some American observers to predict that eventually the U.S. Supreme Court will "conclude that capital punishment and the promise of due process of law are incompatible".[18]

---

[15] Evan J. Mandery, *A Wild Justice: The Death and Resurrection of Capital Punishment in America* (W. W. Norton, 2013), pp. 432–440.

[16] Quoted in Kathleen A. O'Shea, *Women and the Death Penalty in the United States, 1900–1998* (Greenwood Publishing Group, 1999), p. 29.

[17] Austin Sarat, *When the State Kills: Capital Punishment and the American Condition* (Princeton University Press, 2001).

[18] Scott Turow, *Ultimate Punishment: A Lawyer's Reflections on Dealing with the Death Penalty* (Farrar, Straus and Giroux, 2003), p. 114.

In contrast to the United States, there are three reasons why conversion against capital punishment seems unlikely to occur among Justices on Japan's Supreme Court. For one, persons appointed to that Court tend to be more conservative and less ideologically diverse than their counterparts in America.[19] For another, Justices on Japan's Supreme Court serve much shorter terms than American Justices do—an average of 6 years in Japan compared with 26 years in the United States. As a result, Justices in Japan encounter fewer capital cases—and fewer occasions to find flaws in the way capital punishment is administered. Most fundamentally, since death is not "different" in Japanese law, and since "super due process" is not a legal requirement, error is seldom recognized in capital cases (see Chapter 2). By contrast, capital cases have occupied one-quarter to one-half of all state criminal cases on the U.S. Supreme Court's docket in recent years, and nearly half of American death sentences never result in execution because they are reversed on appeal for prosecutorial misconduct, ineffective assistance of counsel, flawed jury instructions, and a host of other errors. In this comparative light, Japanese jurisprudence seems to reflect a perverse principle, that if law aims low in death penalty cases, judges and the general public will seldom be disappointed.

Two Qualifications

Although "public discussion" (*giron*) does not drive death penalty reform, this truth must be qualified in two ways. First, the limited importance of public discussion does not mean the Japanese state should continue withholding information about capital punishment from its citizens, especially in an era when citizens are being asked to make life and death decisions in lay judge trials. As many former lay judges have observed, for *saibanin* to carry out their responsibilities properly, the Ministry of Justice must provide citizens with "all relevant information."[20] As explained in Chapter 3, the secrecy surrounding executions in Japan is deeply disconcerting. It is also more rooted in discretion than

---

[19] J. Mark Ramseyer and Eric B. Rasmusen, *Measuring Judicial Independence: The Political Economy of Judging in Japan* (University of Chicago Press, 2003).

[20] See for example, former lay judge Taguchi Masayoshi, "Shikei to Mukiau Shimin: Saibanin Handan no Hatsushikko o Ukete", *Sekai*, March 2016, pp. 194–199.

law. Officials in the Ministry of Justice (the main architects and enforcers of this secrecy policy) can and should remove this wart from Japan's body politic. The Japanese public deserves more information about how the death penalty is administered even if increased public oversight of executions will not end them, and even if increased transparency is unlikely to change many minds about the propriety of capital punishment. Increased openness is the right thing to do.

The second qualification is that education about the death penalty is not completely futile. As mentioned above, it is most effective when it is directed at the political elites who hold the fate of capital punishment in their hands. The best scholarly work on this subject finds that "the death penalty is always and everywhere an exercise of state power."[21] In this sense, the trajectory of capital punishment is mainly determined by political actors and political processes. The cultural shifts that matter most are those that will influence the attitudes and beliefs of elites (politicians, bureaucrats, and business and legal professionals), by generating discourse among them, by weakening the intensity of support among those who favor retention, and by strengthening the intensity of opposition among those who favor abolition. To the extent that "public discussion" shapes elite opinion in these ways, it can contribute to death penalty reform. Chiba Keiko seemed to recognize this when she advocated the creation of an organ in Parliament to gather and discuss information about the death penalty. Unfortunately, she also saw political action as causally subordinate to "public discussion." Evidence from the rest of the world suggests that she got the dynamic backward.

On Democracy

In sum, belief that "public discussion" (*giron*) will produce death penalty reform contradicts three hard facts. Public opinion about the death penalty is difficult to change in every society. Public opinion about the death penalty in Japan is rooted in moral intuitions about retribution and atonement that are largely impervious to rational discussion. And in other countries, death penalty abolitions and moratoria have been caused by leadership from the front, not by changes in public opinion. But if

---

[21] David Garland, *Peculiar Institution: America's Death Penalty in an Age of Abolition* (The Belknap Press of Harvard University Press, 2010), p. 127.

public discussion in Japan seems unlikely to lead to the end of capital punishment, what hope is there for abolition? Is "leadership from the front" undemocratic or even anti-democratic?

Richard Posner, a prominent federal judge on the U.S. Court of Appeals for the Seventh Circuit in Chicago (who retired from the bench in 2017) and the most cited American legal scholar of all time, claims that the main reason America retains capital punishment long after the developed democracies of Europe abolished it is because America is "more democratic."[22] In his view, American government is permeated with politics, and elected officials find it more necessary to implement policies supported by a majority of voters than do their elected counterparts in countries without an American-style "hyper-democracy" that stresses local decision-making, popular participation, and electoral accountability. Other analysts also conclude that America's "radically local version of democracy" helps explain the persistence of capital punishment in the United States and the "peculiar" forms it takes in many American places.[23]

In Japan, too, prosecutors, politicians, and the public frequently claim that capital punishment is simply an expression of democracy at work.[24] On this view, death sentences and executions are the natural result of majority support for capital punishment. On this view, the death penalty is democratically ordained. And in the context of public support for capital punishment, to oppose it is to defy a central imperative of democratic governance.

Claims that capital punishment reflects "democracy-at-work" are simplistic and misleading, both empirically and theoretically. Empirically, electorates are not well-informed about many political issues, and elections seldom produce governments that are responsive to what (uninformed) voters say they want.[25] What is more, research about "who rules?"

---

[22] Richard Posner, "Capital Crimes", *The New Republic*, April 1, 2002, p. 32.

[23] See, for example, David Garland, *Peculiar Institution: America's Death Penalty in an Age of Abolition* (The Belknap Press of Harvard University Press), p. 309; and Andrew Hammel, *Ending the Death Penalty: The European Experience in Global Perspective* (Palgrave Macmillan, 2010), especially Chapter 8, "Why the European Model Failed in the United States".

[24] Several such claims are discussed in Nempo Shikei Haishi 2017, *Popyurizumu to Shikei* (Impakuto, 2017), pp. 5–64; and in Mai Sato, *The Death Penalty in Japan: Will the Public Tolerate Abolition?* (Springer VS, 2014).

[25] Christopher H. Achen and Larry M. Bartels, *Democracy for Realists: Why Elections Do Not Produce Responsive Governments* (Princeton University Press, 2017).

in democratic countries finds that the views of average people are seldom decisive in policymaking. In the United States, for example, one study tracked how well the preferences of the public and of various groups predicted the ways that Congress and the executive branch would act on 1779 policies over a two-decade period. It found that economic elites and narrow interest groups succeeded in getting their favored policies about half the time, and they succeeded in stopping legislation to which they were opposed nearly all the time. In contrast, mass-based interest groups had little effect on public policy, while the views of ordinary citizens had virtually no effect at all. As the authors of this study concluded, "When the preferences of economic elites and the stands of organized interest groups are controlled for, the preferences of the average American appear to have only a miniscule, near-zero, statistically non-significant impact upon public policy."[26] In Japan as well, organized interest groups and economic elites continue to shape public policy even after the basic rules of the political game have changed.[27]

The main theoretical problem with "democracy at work" claims is that "democracy" means more than majority rule. In fact, there are at least four ways in which "democracy" and the death penalty are related, because democracy can be representative, participatory, legal, or liberal. In *representative democracy*, death penalty policy reflects what citizens want, as indicated in elections, public opinion polls, and other expressions of public sentiment. In *participatory democracy*, the administration of the death penalty allows citizens to perform certain roles in the criminal process, as witnesses, as victims and survivors with a stake in case outcomes, and as lay judges who make life-and-death decisions at trial. In *legal democracy*, the death penalty aims to advance the rule of law by deterring murder and by being administered in a manner that is fair, just, and accurate. And in *liberal democracy*, criminal punishment is supposed to advance values such as dignity, liberty, equality, and the right to life.[28]

---

[26] Martin Gilens and Benjamin I. Page, "Testing Theories of American Politics: Elites, Interest Groups, and Average Citizens", *Perspectives on Politics*, Vol. 12, No. 3 (September 2014), pp. 564–581.

[27] Matthew Carlson, *Money Politics in Japan: New Rules, Old Practices* (Lynne Rienner, 2007).

[28] This analysis relies on the fine work of Maximo Langer and David Alan Sklansky, editors, *Prosecutors and Democracy: A Cross-National Study* (Cambridge University Press, 2017).

As guides for thinking about what democracy requires, these four themes can be seen as different "strands" of democracy that could be tied together in various ways (some thicker than others), or they may be seen as different "lodestars" for guiding the death penalty toward democracy. In either case, discussions of the relationship between democracy and the death penalty in Japan have long been dominated by a narrow understanding of "democracy" that stresses its representative and participatory dimensions while marginalizing its legal and liberal ones. In most discussions, prosecutors, judges, lay judges, and victims are expected to *participate* in the death penalty system as *representatives* who are responsive to public opinion, but little is said about the relevance of legal and liberal values. In this constricted view of democracy, *legal values* such as fairness and due process get discounted or ignored, as do *liberal values* such as human dignity and the right to life. A richer understanding of democracy and the death penalty would not marginalize these legal and liberal values. It would recognize that many of Japan's core values are legal and liberal, and it would acknowledge that the death penalty often undermines them. A richer understanding would also realize that there is wisdom in moving beyond the "tough on crime" (*genbatsuka*) rhetoric that characterizes the culture of capital punishment in Japan, in order to be "smart on crime" (as discussed in Chapter 1, the death penalty does not deter homicide), and in order to respect the rights and dignity of all human beings—even those who have committed terrible crimes.[29]

The abolitions that have occurred in other developed democracies have expressed democratic values—including respect for human rights. I admire former Japanese Minister of Justice Chiba Keiko, who authorized the executions in 2010, but in some ways she has misunderstood the relationship between democracy and death penalty reform—as have many other leaders in Japanese society. Chiba is continuing the struggle to abolish capital punishment, and I believe that, eventually, her side will prevail. After abolition, public support for capital punishment in Japan will probably decline (as it typically does after a country abolishes), Japanese lay judges will no longer be required to make life-and-death decisions, and Japanese victims and survivors will no longer feel the need

---

[29] For an eloquent defense of the right to life in the context of capital punishment, see Yasuda Yoshihiro, *Shikei Bengonin: Ikiru to Iu Kenri* (Kodansha, 2008).

to beg state officials to kill the offenders who have caused their suffering. But until the day of abolition arrives, Japan's leaders need to confront a question that is as fundamental as it has been neglected: Is a reform which permanently deprives a state of the legal authority to kill its own citizens undemocratic?

The Japanese Military and State Killing

For most people most of the time, politics is less a matter of thinking deeply about democracy than it is a matter of social identity and partisan loyalty.[30] Once this fact is recognized, politics can be seen as a parade of symbols and abstractions, and a political analysis will consider how people are placated and aroused by capital punishment.

In Japan, one overlooked aspect of death penalty symbolism is its relation to national defense. Democracy in Japan differs from democracy in other industrial nations because, in several respects, the Japanese state lacks authority to use military power and martial policies.[31] Japan's postwar occupation created a government that is pacifist by constitutional promise (Article 9), pledged neither to threaten force nor use force in international disputes. Of course, Japan's Self Defense Forces are among the most technologically advanced armed forces in the world, and in 2018 the nation's aggregate military expenditures were the ninth highest in the world (just behind Germany and just ahead of South Korea). But when it feels threatened by hostile forces, Japan's constitutional commitment to pacifism removes an important means of governmental assertiveness. For a conservative government, this pacifism in military matters probably feels uncomfortably close to impotence. The restrictions on state killing imposed by Article 9 also help explain why Japan's conservative governments seem determined to carry out executions every year. The constraints of Article 9 make capital punishment a symbol of government power that the country's conservative leaders

---

[30] Jonathan Haidt, *The Righteous Mind: Why Good People Are Divided by Politics and Religion* (Pantheon, 2012).

[31] Sheila A. Smith, *Japan Rearmed: The Politics of Military Power* (Harvard University Press, 2019).

seem loathe to relinquish, for to them it is a potent symbol of state sovereignty and of the proper relationship between the state and its subjects.[32]

Death sentences and executions in Japan declined steadily from the 1950s through the 1980s, but starting in the 1990s, the LDP put increased emphasis on capital punishment as an instrument of government, partly because of the absence of other martial options during a period in which many people (inside Japan and out) were calling on the country to develop a more assertive military posture in order to deal with new threats, such as the rise of China and the provocations of North Korea. Ironically, if the current LDP under Prime Minister Abe Shinzo succeeds in establishing a legal foundation for Japan's military to be more assertive abroad, conservative governments in the future may feel less compelled to promote the symbolic politics of capital punishment at home. There are countries (such as Costa Rica, Iceland, and Liechtenstein) that are pacifist both in military matters and with respect to capital punishment, but they are all significantly smaller than Japan, and they are far less influential internationally. None of them has a history of militarism anything like Japan's effort to create a "Greater East Asia Co-Prosperity Sphere" in the first half of the twentieth century, and most of them abolished the death penalty before they renounced the use of military force. No country as large and powerful as Japan has relinquished both the authority to use military force and the authority to use capital punishment. In this sense, Article 9 could be an obstacle to abolition in Japan. With respect to state killing, Japan is the mirror image of large countries in Europe (such as Germany and France) that retain the right to use military force while renouncing the right to use capital punishment. Time will tell how much longer Japan retains this distinctive status. For the time being, some Japan-watchers will continue to wonder why the Japanese state is permitted to kill its own citizens while it is forbidden to kill foreigners who threaten the nation's peace and welfare.

---

[32] David T. Johnson and Franklin E. Zimring, *The Next Frontier: National Development, Political Change, and the Death Penalty in Asia* (Oxford University Press, 2009), pp. 82–84.

IMAGINING ABOLITION

Although the length of the struggle to end capital punishment in Japan is not known, the outcome seems inevitable in any but the most pessimistic view of the country's future. What circumstances could push Japan toward abolition? Let us imagine two possibilities.

One precipitating cause of abolition could be the clear revelation of a wrongful execution. Wrongful executions were a proximate cause of abolition in Britain in 1965, and in Japan following four death row exonerations in the 1980s, a moratorium on executions ensued for 40 months, from November 1989 to March 1993. But this route to abolition is far from certain, for there was widespread political and public apathy about the risks of wrongful execution after Hakamada Iwao was released from death row in 2014, some 46 years after he was condemned to death. Hakamada's case suggests that even a wrongful execution might result in little political resolve to end capital punishment—or even to substantially reform it. Moreover, prosecutors' resistance to a retrial for Hakamada suggests that they may be willing to deny strong evidence of a wrongful execution if and when it emerges. When power and rationality collide in a legal system, power usually prevails.[33]

A second scenario is that abolition in the United States could stimulate abolition in Japan. The retention of capital punishment in the world's most influential democracy has long helped to legitimate capital punishment in democracies such as Japan, Taiwan, and India. And some analysts believe a nation-wide American abolition could occur in the near future. Professors Carol and Jordan Steiker suggest that "the death penalty will not last much longer in the United States," mainly because many Justices on the U.S. Supreme Court have renounced capital punishment after repeatedly seeing their efforts fail to regulate it in a manner that is consistent with the principles and promises of the U.S. Constitution.[34] Similarly, Professor Brandon Garrett has concluded that American capital punishment "is at the end of its rope." He believes it could be abolished "not in a matter of generations, but in a matter

---

[33] Bent Flyvbjerg, *Rationality and Power: Democracy in Practice* (University of Chicago Press, 1998).

[34] Carol S. Steiker and Jordan M. Steiker, *Courting Death: The Supreme Court and Capital Punishment* (The Belknap Press of Harvard University Press, 2016), pp. 4–5.

of years."[35] And in the U.S. Supreme Court's *Glossip v. Gross* decision (2015), Justice Stephen Breyer (joined by Justice Ruth Bader Ginsburg) stated that he believes it is "highly likely that the death penalty violates the Eighth Amendment" of the U.S. Constitution (prohibiting "cruel and unusual punishment"), because of three constitutional defects in its administration: unreliability in fact-finding, arbitrariness in application, and long delays between death sentences and executions that undermine the death penalty's main penological purposes (deterrence and retribution). Because of these chronic problems, Breyer called for a full briefing before the U.S. Supreme Court on the question of whether American capital punishment violates the Constitution. If such a briefing occurs before a Court with one more member who has serious concerns about the constitutionality of capital punishment than is the case at the time of this writing (July 2019), then American capital punishment could be abolished judicially, with repercussions for Japan and other retentionist nations who will have lost their American cover for a practice that has become increasingly difficult to defend in an era of human rights.

Regardless of the precipitating circumstance, abolition in Japan will occur only if elites push for it. Since conservatives have ruled the country for all but 3 of the last 64 years, we may wonder whether it is realistic to expect a conversion of this kind. Why would conservative policymakers embrace facts (about deterrence and wrongful convictions) they once shunned and adopt a position (abolition) they once abhorred, especially when changing minds on this subject is so difficult? Yet evidence from the United States, where many conservative leaders have turned against mass incarceration and capital punishment, suggests that the right circumstances could produce real reform in Japan too.[36] One key to the conservative turn in America has been a major decline in crime over the past quarter-century, which made it easier for politicians to support "right on crime" policies instead of posturing as "tough on crime." In Japan, crime has been declining for more than a decade, and a once troubling turn toward penal

---

[35] Brandon Garret, *End of Its Rope: How Killing the Death Penalty Can Revive Criminal Justice* (Harvard University Press, 2017), p. 1.

[36] See, for example, David Dagan and Steven M. Teles, *Prison Break: Why Conservatives Turned Against Mass Incarceration* (Oxford University Press, 2016); and George F. Will, "Against the Death Penalty", *Washington Post*, September 28, 2018.

populism has decelerated as incarceration rates have fallen.[37] Time will tell more, but the decline of crime in what is already one of the world's safest societies could eventually prompt some of the country's conservative leaders to embrace "human rights" as a better frame for thinking about capital punishment in the twenty-first century than were the "crime control" and "atonement" frames that they routinely employed in previous decades.[38]

LIFE AFTER DEATH

Let us also imagine what could change in Japan after capital punishment is abolished. This exercise will not only highlight several incentives for abolition; it will reveal some of the effects capital punishment has on other parts of Japan's criminal process. In terms of caseloads, capital punishment is a tiny part of Japan's criminal justice system. Less than 1 percent of all homicide offenders are sentenced to death, and homicide comprises less than 1/1000th of all Penal Code offenses. But capital punishment in Japan attracts far more attention and has many more consequences than its small size seems to warrant. Its disappearance could have at least four positive consequences for Japanese criminal justice, in addition to one consequence that could present a challenge for progressives.[39]

First, the death penalty in Japan promotes the practice of using extreme penal sanctions as status rewards for crime victims and their families. This serves a public relations function for capital punishment, by reducing the discomfort of citizens who worry about the state's power to kill. And pedagogically, the emphasis on punishment as a status reward for victims also implies that the more punishment is administered, the better off victims will be. The use of punishment as a status reward leads ever upward: it

---

[37] David T. Johnson, "Comparative Reflections on American Crime Declines", *Berkeley Journal of Criminal Law*, Issue 23-3 (Fall 2018), pp. 25–45.

[38] Mari Kita and David T. Johnson, "Framing Capital Punishment in Japan: Avoidance, Ambivalence, and Atonement", *Asian Journal of Criminology*, Vol. 9, No. 3 (September 2014), pp. 221–240.

[39] This analysis builds on the fine insights about life after the death penalty in the United States made by Brandon L. Garrett in *End of Its Rope: How Killing the Death Penalty Can Revive Criminal Justice* (Harvard University Press, 2017), pp. 212–260.

is a one-way penal escalator.[40] If 5 years is good, 10 years must be better, and 15 years must be better still. In this way, when criminal punishment is employed as a symbolic currency, the sky is the limit. If Japan abolishes the death penalty, this impulse toward penal inflation would probably decline.

Second, Japan's death penalty provides moral camouflage for other harsh criminal punishments—especially for the increasingly frequent practice of not releasing inmates who have been sentenced to an indefinite term of imprisonment (*muki choeki*). Japan does not have the penalty of life without parole, but in practice, persons sentenced to life with the possibility of parole serve extremely long sentences. As of the end of 2015, 1835 persons were serving a life sentence, which was 15 times more than the number of persons detained on Japan's death rows. Almost half of those "lifers" were over age 60, and 12 had been in prison for more than 50 years. For the past decade, fewer than 10 persons under a life sentence have been released on parole each year.[41] In reality, then, a life sentence in Japan often means "life without parole." If death disappeared as a sentencing option in Japan, a life sentence would be seen for what it is: an extremely severe criminal sanction. And without Japan's punishment ceiling set at death, parole might become a more realistic possibility for persons under a life sentence, and fewer citizens and survivors would have reason to complain that the non-capital sentence some heinous offender received is insufficiently severe.

Third, capital punishment in Japan diverts legal and judicial resources from the scrutiny of other criminal punishments and exercises of state power. Every nation has a limited number of lawyers with the political values and special skills required to defend against government excess in the prohibition of conduct and the punishment of crime. And in nations that retain capital punishment, the ultimate penalty is a magnet for lawyers concerned with excessive governmental power. In Japan, the criminal defense bar is small, and lawyers with this commitment are few and far between. When a significant proportion of the country's best attorneys concentrate

---

[40] Franklin E. Zimring and David T. Johnson, "The Dark at the Top of the Stairs: Four Destructive Influences of Capital Punishment on American Criminal Justice", in Joan Peterselia and Kevin R. Reitz, editors, *The Oxford Handbook of Sentencing and Corrections* (Oxford University Press, 2012), pp. 737–752.

[41] Kanji Muramatsu, David T. Johnson, and Koiti Yano, "The Death Penalty and Homicide Deterrence in Japan", *Punishment & Society*, Vol. 20, No. 4 (October 2018), p. 436 and p. 452.

on capital punishment, the result is a shortage of resources to monitor how state authority is exercised in other realms. Few informed observers believe Japan's bar performs adequately as a watchdog over state power (the task is large and the bar is small). Abolition of capital punishment would enable more progressive "cause lawyers" to confront criminal, constitutional, and regulatory issues where their help is sorely needed.[42]

Fourth, the end of capital punishment could bring political benefits to Japan, both domestically and internationally. At home, debates about criminal justice policy are frequently distorted by the power of capital punishment to command public attention and political concern. The abolition of capital punishment would eliminate this distortion and enable more frequent assessments of other criminal justice problems, such as the power of police, the discretion of prosecutors, and the deference of judges to law enforcement. Abolition would also reduce tensions between Japan and its international peers, especially the rich and democratic countries of Europe, which frequently complain about Japan's unwillingness to regard capital punishment as a human rights issue.[43] And the disappearance of the death penalty would permit Japan to avoid claims of hypocrisy when it criticizes countries such as China and North Korea for their human rights failures. In the long run, the abolition of capital punishment in Japan could even change the nation's self-conception, from that of a country and culture that are ambivalent about state killing ("no" to war but "yes" to capital punishment) to one that stands consistently in support of life.

Research shows that American states that abolish capital punishment do not experience the "parade of horribles" that death penalty proponents predict. In the six American states that abolished between 2007 and 2014, murder rates in general did not increase, and neither did murder rates of police officers and correctional officials who were killed in the line of duty.[44] There is little reason to suppose murder

---

[42] Daniel H. Foote, "Cause Lawyering in Japan: Reflections on the Case Studies and Justice Reform", in Patricia G. Steinhoff, editor, *Going to Court to Change Japan: Social Movements and the Law in Contemporary Japan* (University of Michigan Center for Japanese Studies, 2014), pp. 165–180.

[43] Sangmin Bae, "Friends Do Not Let Friends Execute: The Council of Europe and the International Campaign to Abolish the Death Penalty", *International Politics*, Vol. 45, No. 2 (March 2008), pp. 129–145.

[44] American Bar Association Committee on Capital Punishment, "Life After the Death Penalty: Implications for Retentionist States", August 14, 2017, pp. 1–34, at https://files.deathpenaltyinfo.org/legacy/files/pdf/Life-After-Death-Penalty_Transcript.pdf.

rates in Japan would rise after abolition, but abolition could have another unwelcome effect, by removing the spotlight that capital punishment shines on the workings of Japanese criminal justice. Death is a special criminal sanction, even if Japanese courts are reluctant to recognize this as a matter of law. Its severity and its irrevocability evoke heightened concern about the possibility of justice miscarrying. One effect of capital punishment in Japan is public and media attention on problems in criminal justice that might otherwise escape notice. If death is abolished as a criminal sanction, Japanese progressives may need to find new ways to concentrate attention on the serious problems that afflict the criminal justice system more broadly. I believe abolition will eventually occur in Japan—and I hope concern about the country's wrongful conviction problem will increase in the era of life after death.

Open Access This chapter is licensed under the terms of the Creative Commons Attribution-NonCommercial-NoDerivatives 4.0 International License (http://creativecommons.org/licenses/by-nc-nd/4.0/), which permits any noncommercial use, sharing, distribution and reproduction in any medium or format, as long as you give appropriate credit to the original author(s) and the source, provide a link to the Creative Commons license and indicate if you modified the licensed material. You do not have permission under this license to share adapted material derived from this chapter or parts of it.

The images or other third party material in this chapter are included in the chapter's Creative Commons license, unless indicated otherwise in a credit line to the material. If material is not included in the chapter's Creative Commons license and your intended use is not permitted by statutory regulation or exceeds the permitted use, you will need to obtain permission directly from the copyright holder.

Index

A
Abe, Shinzo (Prime Minister of Japan), 114
abolition, 2, 3, 5–11, 13–15, 17, 59, 82, 92, 96, 102–104, 106, 109, 112–117, 119, 120
accuracy (factual and moral), 63, 97, 98
acquittal, 23, 66, 69, 70, 72, 73
Akabori, Masao, 71
Aoki, Keiko, 70
Aristotle, 97
Article 9 of the Japanese constitution, 113, 114
Article 36 of the Japanese constitution, 52, 53, 55, 56
Asahara, Shoko, 3
atonement, 16, 55, 93, 105, 109, 117
Aum Shinrikyo, v, vii–ix, 40

B
bad faith, vi
Bae, Sangmin, 9, 104, 119

Blackmun, Harry (U.S. Supreme Court Justice), 34, 35
Blackstone, William, 63
Boku, Tatsuhiro, 70
botched executions, 17, 52, 82
Britain, 6, 9, 115
burden (*futan*), 97

C
Callins v Collins (1994), 35
Camus, Albert, vii, 44
Chesterton, G.K., 98, 99
Chiang, Kuo-ching, 17
Chiba, Keiko (Minister of Justice), 9, 41, 101–104, 107, 109, 112
China (People's Republic of), 17
closure, 92, 93
confessions, 53, 65, 72, 73, 78, 86, 90
Conspiracy at Matsukawa (book), 73
Conviction integrity unit (CIUs), 78
conviction rate, 69, 85, 86, 99
culture, 3, 49, 50, 63, 74, 75, 90, 96, 97, 112, 119

culture of denial (*hitei no bunka*), 4, 63, 74, 75, 78, 79, 82

D
Darrow, Clarence, 22
"death is different", 21, 95
death row, 5, 27, 38, 40, 41, 48, 49, 55, 63–65, 71, 74, 78, 79, 115, 118
death sentencing rates, 33, 86
defense lawyers, 3, 20–23, 28–30, 32, 39, 41, 53, 55, 56, 60, 63, 70, 74, 84, 86–90, 92, 93, 99
DeLuna, Carlos, 65
democracy, 2, 3, 5, 47, 74, 95, 110–113, 115
"democracy at work", 110, 111
Democratic Party of Japan (DPJ), 6, 8, 9, 101, 102
deterrence, 11–13, 16, 58, 116
discovery of evidence, 74
DNA evidence, 64

E
emotions (at murder trials), 95
Europe, 2, 5–7, 11, 67, 110, 114, 119
execution, 2–5, 7–9, 11, 12, 16, 17, 21, 23, 24, 27, 37–41, 44–60, 62, 63, 65, 66, 76, 81, 82, 92, 95, 101–104, 107–110, 112–116

F
final words, 49, 50, 87, 94
Foote, Daniel H., 32, 69, 71, 73, 86, 88, 90, 119
"forgivable cruelty" (and hanging), 56
Forum 90, 3
Fox, Michael H., 70
France, 6, 9, 67, 114
Furman v. Georgia (1972), 2, 32, 105

G
Gardner v. Florida (1977), 94
Garland, David, ix, 2, 7, 15, 16, 38, 46, 94, 109, 110
Garrett, Brandon L., 64, 82, 115, 117
Germany, 6, 8, 14, 47, 59, 66, 67, 113, 114
Ginsburg, Ruth Bader, 116
Glossip v. Gross (2015), 116
Goto, Sadato, 56
Gouda, Mamora, 3
Gregg v. Georgia (1976), 2, 33, 105, 107

H
Hakamada, Iwao, 61–65, 68, 72–74, 78, 79, 115
Hammel, Andrew, 2, 6, 15, 104, 110
hanging, 8, 12, 27, 30, 31, 39–41, 45–48, 50–59, 102, 103
Hayashi, Ikuo, vii
Herber, Erik, 83, 91
Higuchi, Hiroaki, 29
Hirano, Ryuichi, 32, 88, 89
Holmes, Sherlock, 87
homicide, 3, 6, 7, 11–13, 23, 24, 48, 64–67, 85, 89, 90, 92, 94, 106, 112, 117
Hood, Roger, 10, 13, 24, 96
Horikawa, Keiko, 3, 26, 55, 57, 102, 103
Hoyle, Carolyn, 10, 13, 96
"humane" executions, 45, 46, 56, 58
human rights, 2, 9, 10, 14, 17, 21, 69, 96, 97, 102, 112, 116, 117, 119

I
India, 9, 10, 14, 46, 115
Ino, Kazuo, 25, 27, 28
interrogation, 62, 72, 73, 76, 84, 89
Ishikawa, Kazuo, 64

J
Japan Innocence & Death Penalty Information Center, 70
Johnson, Chalmers, 73
judges, 4, 16, 20, 21, 23–29, 31, 32, 34, 45, 49, 52, 54–57, 60, 62, 64, 66, 70, 72–76, 78, 82–88, 90, 93, 94, 96–99, 106–108, 110–112, 119
Jury Act (prewar Japan), 83

K
Karenina principle, 1, 2, 17
kessai (hierarchical consultation and approval), 69
"kidnap justice" (*hitojichi shiho*), 84
Kim, Sung-woon (film director), 64
Kita, Mari, 105, 117
Kitani, Akira, 70

L
lay judge system (*saibanin seido*), 25, 26, 83, 85
leadership from the front, 17, 104, 109, 110
legal democracy, 111, 112
legislature, 54, 56
Leopard, The (novel), 71
liberal democracy, 10, 111, 112
Liberal Democratic Party, 8, 10
Liebman, James S., 22, 23, 65, 66
life sentence (*muki choeki*), 3, 118
life without parole, 24, 54, 118

M
MacArthur, Douglas, 47
Mainali, Govinda, 70
manga, 3
Marshall hypothesis, 32, 84, 106, 107

Marshall, Thurgood, 32, 84, 105
Matsumoto (Japan), v
Menda, Sakae, 38, 71
mental illness (on death row), viii
military (Japan), 113, 114
Ministry of Justice (Japan), 40, 41, 45, 54, 102, 103, 108
miscarriage of justice, 63
Miyazawa, Setsuo, 73, 84, 86, 98
moral camouflage, 118
moratorium (on executions), 8, 82, 115
Murai, Hiroaki, 20
Murakami, Haruki, vi
Muraki, Atsuko, 71
Muramatsu, Kanji, 11, 118

N
Nagata, Kenji, 3, 26, 47, 48, 50, 52, 54, 57, 58
Nagayama (death sentencing standards), 26
Nakagawa, Tomomasa, 46, 54
National Police Agency (Japan), 11, 76

O
Obara-Minnitt, Mika, 82
Occupation of Japan, 8
Ogata, Hidenori, 102
Ogawa, Toshio (Minister of Justice), 9
Orwell, George, 102

P
participatory democracy, 111
penal inflation, 118
Peters, Karl, 66
pivotal question (regarding capital punishment), ix

police, 23, 62–64, 72, 73, 75–78, 84, 87, 88, 119
politics, 7, 9, 75, 99, 109, 110, 113, 114
positive functions of capital punishment, 15, 16
Posner, Richard, 110
Powell, Lewis, 33, 107
Prosecution Review Commission (Japan), 84, 85
prosecutors, 11, 15, 20, 21, 23–26, 30, 31, 40, 46, 52, 54, 55, 57, 61–64, 66, 68–79, 83–89, 91–95, 98, 99, 103, 106, 110, 112, 115, 119
public discussion (*giron*), 45, 57, 103, 106–109
public opinion, 4, 6, 9, 13, 15, 59, 99, 103–105, 109, 111, 112

R
Rabl, Walter, 46, 54
recording (interrogations), 73, 74, 84
representative democracy, 111
resources, legal and judicial, 118, 119
restorative justice, 91
retention, 3, 5–7, 9, 10, 16, 47, 106, 109, 115
retrial, 23, 27, 48, 62, 64, 68, 72, 115
retribution, 13, 16, 95, 105, 109, 116
revenge, 8, 13, 52, 95, 96
rough justice, 26

S
Saito, Sachio, 71
Sakamoto, Toshio, 38, 39
Sakamoto, Tsutsumi, v
Sakurai, Shoji (Fukawa case), 64, 70
Sarat, Austin, 7, 10, 33, 34, 38, 39, 46, 58, 59, 107

Sato, Mai, 15, 45, 104–106, 110
Schmidt, Petra, 11, 53
Schulz, Kathryn, 75, 79
secrecy, 13, 16, 17, 21, 29, 31, 38, 41, 44–49, 55, 60, 76, 77, 102, 108
"self-sufficiency", 10
shincho (caution about capital punishment), 74
Shinomiya, Satoru, 83, 84
Shinozawa, Kazuo, 102
silence, 13, 21, 31, 38, 41, 47, 58, 73, 89, 103
Simon, Dan, 62, 66, 67
South Korea, 5, 9, 14, 104, 113
spiritual advisors, 39
"stable feelings" (*shinjo no antei*), 40
Steiker, Carol S., 2, 22, 33, 106, 115
Steiker, Jordan M., 2, 22, 115
Steinhoff, Patricia G., 72, 119
Stevens, John Paul, 15, 33, 107
Stewart, Potter, 33, 107
Sugaya, Toshikazu, 64, 70
Sugiyama, Takao (Fukawa case), 64, 70
Suo, Masayuki, 71, 73, 87
super due process, 21, 22, 24, 32, 35, 107, 108
Supreme Court, Japan, 19, 20, 26, 27, 30–32, 34, 45, 46, 53, 57, 59, 79, 82, 108
Supreme Court, U.S., 2, 21, 32, 34, 82, 84, 94, 105, 107, 108, 115, 116
"surprise attack" (*damashi-uchi*), 38
survivors, 13, 16, 21, 25, 56, 83, 91–93, 95, 111, 112, 118

T
Tagusari, Maiko, 4, 91
Taiwan, 9, 14, 17, 104, 115
Takami, Sunao, 30, 52–57

Takano, Takashi, 28, 29, 70, 86, 90, 98
Takeda, Masahiro, 85, 106
Taki, Makoto (Minister of Justice), 9
Taniguchi, Shigeyoshi, 71
Tateyama, Tatsumi, 20, 21, 25, 26, 28, 30
Temkin, Moshik, 2, 14
time (and executions), 5, 11, 16, 38, 48, 50
Tokyo War Crimes Trial, 8, 47
Tolstoy, Leo, 1
"tough on crime" (*genbatsuka*), 112, 116
Tsuchimoto, Takeshi, 54, 55, 57
Turow, Scott, ix, 7, 35, 92, 95, 107

U

unavoidable (*yamu o enai*), 45, 56, 77
Urazaki, Hiroyasu, 20

V

Vanoverbeke, Dimitri, 83
vengeance, culture of, 93, 96, 97

via negativa, 17
victim participation system, 4, 25, 83, 91, 94, 97
victims, 4, 11, 13, 16, 21, 25, 26, 39, 56, 63, 64, 69, 85, 89, 91–98, 111, 112, 117

W

wrongful convictions, 4, 16, 17, 58, 62–75, 77–79, 82, 116, 120

Y

Yamaguchi, Susumu, 21, 31, 32
Yanagihara, Hiroshi, 70
Yano, Koiti, 11, 118
Yasuda, Yoshihiro, 3, 112

Z

Zimring, Franklin E., 2, 6, 9, 12, 33, 93, 104, 114, 118

The manufacturer's authorised representative in the EU is Springer Nature Customer Service Centre GmbH, Europaplatz 3, 69115 Heidelberg, Germany. If you have any concerns regarding our products, please contact ProductSafety@springernature.com

Printed and bound by CPI Group (UK) Ltd, Croydon, CR0 4YY

23/03/2026

02076447-0008